NARRATIVE Bʏ ɴᴜᴍʙᴇʀѕ

As jobs become increasingly similar, there are two skills that everyone needs if they're going to thrive. These are the ability to interrogate and make sense of data, and the ability to use insights extracted from data to persuade others to act. Analytics + storytelling = influence.

Humans are hardwired to respond to stories and story structure. Stories are how we make sense of and navigate the world. We respond best to stories that are based on evidence. But storytellers need to use data as the foundation of stories, not as the actual stories themselves. To be truly impactful, rational facts need to be presented with a veneer of emotion.

The Big Data revolution means more data is available than ever. The trouble is, most people aren't very numerate or good at statistics. Many find it hard to look at data and extract insights. Meanwhile, those for whom numbers hold no fear don't always make the best storytellers. They mistakenly believe they need to prove their point by showing their workings.

There are some simple and effective rules of data-driven storytelling that help everyone tell more compelling, evidence-based stories, whoever they need to convince. *Narrative by Numbers* shows you how.

Sam Knowles is a corporate storyteller with 30 years' experience helping businesses communicate better. Originally a classicist, he holds a doctorate in psychology, the source of his understanding of human motivation and his passion for data-driven stories. His purpose is to make businesses sound human.

We need this book! Evidence and numbers help us to make sense of the world, to transcend how things appear, and find out how they really are. But this is not a technical journey – it's a human one, of meanings and relationships, and Sam Knowles shows why we need to grasp that first. With an armful of words, a poet crafts meaning or passion or action. But what do we do with an armful of statistics? Sam Knowles has the answers.

Tracey Brown, Director, Sense About Science

Numbers aren't the enemy of narrative – quite the opposite. Relevant data should be the foundation stones of stories with impact. This approach is clearly relevant for the research and insights business, but also today for every kind of organisation: public, private, and third sector. Sam Knowles makes the case for storytelling by numbers powerfully and persuasively, while at the same time offering a clear how-to guide. To be recommended.

Lord Cooper of Windrush, Founder, Populus

We live in a world of uncertainty. What and who can we trust – and how will we know? Sam Knowles helps to unravel today's biggest question. His thesis – that data is a trusted friend which provides life's "True North" and the certainty we yearn for – is compelling.

Michael Greenlees, "Godfather of London advertising",
Founder, Chairman & CEO of Gold Greenlees Trott

John Naisbitt, author of *Megatrends*, said: "We are drowning in information but starved for knowledge." Today, we are drowning in data and starving for wisdom. In this book, Sam Knowles teaches us skills that are practical and easily applied to make sense of data that every marketer needs.

Bharat Avalani, Former Unilever marketer;
storyteller and memory collector

People who are good with words are seldom good with numbers and vice versa – or so conventional wisdom has it. Sam Knowles appears to be very good at both. His book is a persuasive case for why combining narrative and numbers is essential in an age of big data and short messages. I will be recommending it to my students.

Professor Trevor Morris, Richmond University

Sam's book is the perfect embodiment of the principles he uncovers and outlines. He looks at and makes sense of the data, and weaves it into a story that is both convincing and inspiring. He ably demonstrates his central premise: analytics plus storytelling equals influence. And with this book: QED. Essential reading for anyone in the insight industry, or anyone who has written or sat through an interminable presentation of loosely related data points and cried out for some story to make sense of it all.

Jem Fawcus, Founder & Group CEO, Firefish

Over the last several years many books have been written to help organizations make sense of marketing data. Unfortunately for those marketers and communicators on the front lines, many of those books were written with the analyst in mind. That angle, while valuable for the analysts, dismisses the people who need to use data the most. The good news for that audience is that Sam Knowles has been in their shoes many times before and brings that perspective to *Narrative by Numbers*. Sam presents an excellent overview and guide for how marketers can utilize data to tell better stories within their organizations. The framework that Sam presents will allow you to understand marketing performance, grow your budget and expand your influence within the organization. It is a must read.

Chuck Hemann, Author

The thesis of this book is spot on. Storytelling has been a defining part of humanity since we came down from the trees, sat in front of the fire, and painted caves. With the abundance of data that surrounds us all today, our stories have the potential to be that much more relevant and powerful.

Michael Karg, Group CEO, Ebiquity

The wealth of information that swirls around corporations today also threatens to overwhelm them. But if the right data is captured and it's analyzed in the right way, the insights extracted truly can drive corporate strategy. Sam's approach to storytelling with statistics as the starting point is both practical and actionable. This is a polished primer from a seasoned practitioner.

Chris Deri, President, Teneo Digital

This book is the 101 for anyone who wants their insights to shine. Sam guides the reader on an engaging journey, from data to impactful delivery, by explaining the methods to craft a data driven story.

Tim Ward, Head of Analytics, Square Enix West

Analytics is so important in guiding decision-making and turning insights into action. But drowning your audience with facts and numbers is a real turn-off. Turning these numbers into stories is the way to engage people – consumers as well as customers and employees – making them real and tangible and injecting them with relevant emotionality. Sam knows how to achieve this with impact, and this book shows you how.

Vera Markl-Moser, Global Sustainable Business
Development Director, Unilever

The separate worlds of art and science merge in the masterful hands of Sam Knowles as he expertly guides us into understanding how to find the art in the science. This hugely important book is essential reading for communicators, scientists, academics, and anyone who needs to understand how to find stories in the numbers.

Tim Johns, Business Coach and former Head
of Communications for Sainsbury's, BT, and Unilever

The Big Data revolution has confused the world's communicators for too long. What really matters is the relatively small and self-contained neighbourhood of relevant data. Sam's book shows organisations what to look for, what to avoid, and how to exploit the power of data to tell engaging and impactful stories.

Neville Hobson, Social Media Strategist at the Internet Society

For as long as we can remember, data merchants and storytellers have been quite content to plough their separate fields – the storytellers wanted no truck with numbers while the data merchants remained blissfully ignorant of the power of the narrative. With *Narrative by Numbers*, Sam Knowles has shattered this cosy co-existence and produced a timely synergy of hard data and storyline. Like an ingenious alchemist, he's succeeded in fusing together two elements that once occupied very separate worlds. In the process he's created a new and explosive compound, the reverberations of which we're going to hear for many years to come.

Dr Peter Collett, Psychologist and Body Language Expert,
University of Oxford, UK

NARRATIVE BY NUMBERS

How to Tell Powerful and Purposeful Stories with Data

SAM KNOWLES

APRIL 2019

Routledge
Taylor & Francis Group

LONDON AND NEW YORK

First published 2018
by Routledge
2 Park Square, Milton Park, Abingdon, Oxon OX14 4RN

and by Routledge
711 Third Avenue, New York, NY 10017

Routledge is an imprint of the Taylor & Francis Group, an informa business

British Library Cataloguing-in-Publication Data
A catalogue record for this book is available from the British Library

Library of Congress Cataloging-in-Publication Data
A catalog record has been requested for this book

ISBN: 978-0-8153-5315-7 (hbk)
ISBN: 978-0-8153-5314-0 (pbk)
ISBN: 978-1-351-13722-5 (ebk)

Typeset in Joanna Sans
by Apex CoVantage, LLC

CONTENTS

ACKNOWLEDGEMENTS AND INSPIRATIONS

Narrative by Numbers may have one author, but it has many interested cousins, some of them several times removed.

The idea for a book came up during my first coaching session – as a coaching guinea pig – with the splendid **Tim Johns**. Tim has been a client, will always be a mentor, and morphed into a coach when he decided to train as one. I had six brilliant sessions for the price of none as he learned his coaching trade. He became progressively less directive over our year working together, just after I'd set up my corporate and brand storytelling business, Insight Agents. But at the end of our first session, he said: "If you want to become Mr Data-Driven Storyteller, if you want to give a TED talk, it's simple. You have to write the book. Get to it." So here it is. We'll see about the TED . . .

My wife, life, and business partner **Saskia**, with whom I've already spent more than half my life (we got together on the first day of the second term of our first year at university). I've been saying I'm going to write a book – on comedy, on my father, on insight – since almost the first day we met. Saskia's sense of reality, tinged with a very helpful dose of scepticism, has always kept me honest. So here it is at last, my darling.

Dr Beth Miller, my writing coach. OK, I don't pay her (all the time) to help with my writing, but she's been a true inspiration. First for getting her novels (and non-fiction, including the excellent Archers and Shakespeare handbooks) published and selling. Second, for the unforgettable course "Get Going On Your Book Before Christmas" in autumn 2014. Third, for telling me that the only way to write a book is to write a book – no excuses. And fourth, for suggesting that I set up a Writing Group with other writers, to share and critique work and frustrations between us.

Derek Allen, **Annie Mackey**, and **Lulah Ellender**, the other members of my Writing Group. We meet every now and again, usually over the legendary jerk chicken (for me at least) at the Lewes Arms, and together we make a great mutual support network. Your stories of the Jews in Denmark during World War II, self-discovery in the Australian outback against a backdrop of parental madness, and finding yourself and your mother via your grandmother's lists are all inspirational. And it's all down to you three – especially Lulah – that I've written *Narrative by Numbers* first and as the prequel to *How to Be Insightful*, which I've been working on since 2014 and will follow soon. Promise.

Stuart Lotherington, Senior Partner at SBR Consulting. One of the most inspiring and impactful trainers I've ever come across. After attending a consultative sales training course with SBR in 2012 that fundamentally changed my outlook on how to do business, I occasionally attend their free taster sessions in Covent Garden's Connaught Rooms. In early January 2016, Stuart ran a workshop on goal setting, and his ten-point, goal-setting framework is what finally gave me the stimulus to write this thing.

And lastly to my son and shareholder in the family business, **Max**, whose love of puns, and playing with language, and storytelling since he could speak, are just three of a thousand things about him that make me laugh and love and smile every day. His edit of an early draft of Chapter 1 was brutal, but spot on.

To you all, thanks for the inspiration. The mistakes – as ever – are the sub-editor's.

PREFACE: ANALYTICS + STORYTELLING = INFLUENCE

The two core skills required to thrive in the knowledge economy are analytics and storytelling. I wrote this book to explain how important and yet straightforward it is to combine these two skills. And to show how impactful and influential you can be if you can successfully weave narratives that are data-driven by design.

It is my intention that *Narrative by Numbers* should be instructive, entertaining, and at the same time intensely practical. While the rules and guidance contained in these pages could never hope to be definitive and would never pretend to be so, my aspiration is that those charged with being data-driven storytellers are likely to exceed their peers' and bosses' expectations if they follow the advice set out here.

Each topic chapter includes an example of a data-driven story from the public eye over the past decade or so, stories that have moved individuals to action and in some cases mobilised millions. And each topic chapter also concludes with a practical exercise designed to reinforce the lessons learned and rules extracted, each one tried and tested in the training sessions I run. For there's little point of theory without practice, just as, for me, there's little point of stories without data, woven into a narrative.

To support this book and its mission to help the world's data-driven storytellers become more impactful yet, we've created a website called www.narrativebynumbers.com. Swing by, pull up a virtual chair, and become part of the community. It'll be great to have you along and hear the tales you have to tell.

I trust you find this book and its site helpful.

1

THE TWO SKILLS EVERYONE NEEDS TODAY

> *[Nobel laureate] Lord Rutherford used to tell his staff at the Cavendish Laboratory that if they couldn't explain their physics to a barmaid, it was bad physics.*
>
> David Ogilvy (1963), *Confessions of an Advertising Man*

FIRST PRINCIPLES

There are two skills that everyone needs in today's knowledge economy to thrive and do their jobs most effectively. These are the ability to interrogate, understand, and extract meaning from data and statistics, and the ability to use the insights derived from the data to move people to action. Analytics + storytelling = influence. The purpose of this book is to show you how to excel at both and make the combination worth very much more than the sum of the parts. We're here to understand how to develop narrative by numbers.

We are all, in the words of U.S. business writer Dan Pink in his book *To Sell Is Human*, in the "moving business". And the best way to persuade, inspire, and convince others to do something is to bring together analytics and storytelling: to make data and statistics the foundation stones of the stories you tell. The impact of combining analytics with storytelling holds good for most everyone working in the public or private sector; in commerce, finance, or government; in academia, medicine, or education.

The data generated by and available to everyone in all stripes of organisation has grown exponentially in recent years, and the social media revolution means that today many more voices matter in the public domain. In one capacity or another, both formally and informally, more and more individuals have responsibility for speaking for or as an organisation. These trends show little sign of slowing down, which means the ostensibly fire-and-ice ability to tell impactful stories rooted in data and statistics will be everybody's business within no more than ten years.

In caricature, the data analyst is an introverted, self-reliant number-cruncher who has better relationships with machines than he – and it's always he in the stereotype – does with other people. He's got a brain the size of the planet and colleagues consider him to be a social liability to be kept away from clients at all costs, but the insights he can generate with data can help unlock the challenge at hand. There are also often pointed (and usually groundless) snidey sideswipes at the analyst for his attention to personal hygiene, be it showering, shaving, or skincare.

And in caricature, the raconteur is an extraverted, entertaining, empathetic figure who comes alive in a roomful of people and who can use the power of storytelling to convince anyone to do anything. Even Inuit to buy ice, Geordies to buy coal, and Athenians – as the clichés have it – to buy owls. Colleagues and friends talk warmly about storytellers, and while in business their appearance may be protected or rationed – well, you wouldn't want too much of a good thing, would you? – when the meeting is set, it's one not to be missed.

The truth about both capabilities and the archetypal individuals who best exemplify them is rather more nuanced and prosaic.

THE TROUBLE WITH EDUCATION

Twenty or thirty years ago, it was fashionable in education systems around the world to classify students as either artists or scientists. I know because – in Britain at least – I was there. It was the done thing to channel people as early as 14 or 15 to pursue one path or the other. This would dictate choices of subjects for the last two years of school, which would in turn dictate choices of degree courses and, inevitably, career trajectory. If you didn't do chemistry, physics, and maths for your final school exams, it was very hard to see you progressing far in the chemical engineering world.

Unfortunately, it became a badge of honour among many of those artists – who found mathematics to be a challenge and so gave it up as soon as they were not much more than numerate – to happily admit they were "no good" at the subject. Perversely, it even became a little bit cool to say so, too. This problem was first formally identified in 1959 by C.P. Snow in his Rede lecture at Cambridge titled "The Two Cultures". Snow was both a novelist and a physical chemist – a Renaissance man and data-driven storyteller, if ever there was one – and his lecture proposed that the forced separation of the humanities and the sciences would prevent the world from solving its most pressing challenges. His diagnosis of the challenge is so well expressed, it's worth repeating this line of argument:

> *A good many times I have been present at gatherings of people who, by the standards of the traditional culture, are thought highly educated and who have, with considerable gusto, been expressing their incredulity at the illiteracy of scientists. Once or twice I have been provoked and have asked the company how many of them could describe the Second Law of Thermodynamics. The response was cold: it was also negative. Yet I was asking something which is about the scientific equivalent of: "Have you read a work of Shakespeare's?" I now believe that if I had asked an even simpler question – such as, "What do you mean by mass, or acceleration?", which is the scientific equivalent of saying, "Can you read?" – not more than one in ten of the highly educated would have felt that I was speaking the same language. So, the great edifice of modern physics goes up, and the majority of the cleverest people in the western world have about as much insight into it as their Neolithic ancestors would have had.*

Inspired by Snow's lecture, early 1960s satirists Michael Flanders and Donald Swann painted a caricatured picture of how those schooled in the humanities need to talk to scientists if they want to make themselves understood. In the introduction to their song *The First and Second Law of Thermodynamics*, Flanders addresses an imaginary scientist with the line: "Ah, H_2SO_4 Professor. Don't synthesize anything I wouldn't synthesize. Oh, and the reciprocal of pi to your good wife."

Today, fortunately, the impact of early choices is being mitigated to an extent by broader advanced level subject arrays – particularly thanks to innovations such as the International Baccalauréat. It's encouraging seeing the Arts trying to jimmy themselves among Science, Technology, Engineering, and Maths, and to see that STEM subjects are morphing into STEAM.

The fact that jobs are, indeed, becoming more similar also helps. Because, increasingly, we are all in the moving business, to thrive in this new world order we all need to master the skills of analytics and storytelling.

THE TROUBLE WITH PSYCHOLOGY

Psychology also needs to shoulder some of the blame for the misperception that analytics and storytelling are not easy bedfellows – or at least the wilful misinterpretation of some influential psychological research. It is still widely believed, for instance, that these two core skills are mediated by different hemispheres or sides of the brain.

Humans are simple creatures, albeit simple creatures in possession of the most powerful supercomputer yet devised or discovered: the human brain. I say we are simple creatures because we tend to look for simple, elegant, and reductive solutions to the challenges that face us. We also use a wide array of shortcuts – technically known as cognitive heuristics – to try to solve these challenges. While heuristics enable us to make decisions when confronted with mountains of data, they often lead us to make very predictable mistakes in data processing and decision-making under pressure or uncertainty. This has been characterised as System 1 thinking by the psychologist Daniel Kahneman in his popular 2011 book *Thinking, Fast and Slow*, in contrast to more deliberative, considered, and slower System 2 thinking. That book summarises decades of Kahneman's research, including the award-winning experiments he ran with his long-time collaborator, Amos Tversky.

A good example of this process in action is the universal human desire to favour single-factor solutions – solutions that say that "the Gulf War was about oil", that "Leicester City won the premiership because of Claudio Ranieri's leadership", or that "Trump won the 2016 election because of fake news". When we're generalists looking into a specialist field, as most of us are most of the time considering most issues, we find it very difficult to consider the interaction of multiple factors working together. Factors like: Ranieri's management style, plus Vardy, Mahrez, and Kanté all peaking in the same team at the same time, plus the Premiership's Big Six clubs all underperforming for different reasons in the 2015/16 season, plus Jose Mourinho imploding and being sacked by Chelsea, plus the impact of the Sky billions on smaller clubs' playing budgets, plus media momentum, plus bookmakers' commentary, plus, plus, plus . . .

When it comes to popular neuroscience – a dangerous oxymoron if ever there was one – the left brain/right brain, analytical/intuitive, sciences/arts, rational/emotional dichotomy has proved to be one of the most stubborn and pervasive and inaccurate separations of function yet perpetrated by psychology on its lay readers. It's a complete caricature, and a convenient single-factor explanation of the ultimate supercomputer that is the human brain. It is, in the handle of one of my favourite Twitter feeds, total @neurobollocks. And it's been popularised at every turn by the reductionist, popular media.

Yes, it's true that certain functions more connected with analytical processing have been identified as generating more left than right brain activity. But to ascribe this function to a single hemisphere and to categorise individuals as left- or right-brained on this basis is to display gross ignorance of the finer-grained nature of the brain.

Computer/brain analogies are always imperfect. This is because the billions of neurons and junctions between them – the synapses – not to mention the hundreds of different neurotransmitters at work simultaneously, independently and on each other, are generations more complex than any computer made by humans to date. Or for the foreseeable future.

Talking about the impact of brain damage on brain function, the psychologist Richard Gregory[1] drew a famous analogy: "If I remove a transistor from a radio and the result is that the only sound that I can get out of a radio is a howl, I am not entitled to conclude that the function of the transistor in the intact radio is as a howl suppressor."

Just as a transistor is not a howl suppressor, so the left hemisphere is not responsible for analytics nor the right brain storytelling. Complex brain function like analytics requires the simultaneous and sequential firing and interaction of hundreds or more of interconnected functional units controlling discrete subroutines. These exist across both hemispheres. It would be convenient if the generalist, lay public could understand the left brain as the analytical part of the brain and the right as the storytelling part, but only convenient because it would tell a simple, reductionist story. And as Steven Pinker frustratingly concludes in his 1997 book, *How the Mind Works*, as creatures we lack the cognitive architecture to understand the promise of the title of his book. Frustratingly, but – it appears – quite correctly.

The other glaring error of the left brain/right brain, analytics/storytelling division of both function and types of people is that it assumes that the other hemisphere (and functionality) is inactive. So, analysts can't communicate, and communicators can't analyse. While it's true that some people are naturally better at analysis than others, and others are naturally better storytellers, as jobs in the knowledge economy converge and as we all gravitate towards the "moving business", we are all required to excel across both domains. And the motive of this drive is a little word with a big impact on all our lives. Data.

THE RISE AND RISE OF DATA

Data has grown so fast and to such an extent that it's rarely talked about these days as just plain old data. Today it's usually big data. And though English resists the temptation to follow its Germanic cousins and capitalise words or phrases other than names, countries, or brands, big data is also very often Big Data. Perhaps it's grown so much, it's already acquired titular or nation status.

It's hard to keep a handle on how much data individuals, businesses, and nations produce, and many find the sheer volume of data available today to be overpowering – threatening, even. In *Big Data: A Revolution That Will Transform How We Live, Work, and Think*, Viktor Mayer-Schönberger and Kenneth Cukier calculated that, by the end of 2013, there were an estimated 1,200 exabytes (EB) of data stored on earth. 1EB is 10^18bytes. Or 1bn GB, enough to fill 40bn, 32GB iPads, which would stretch from the Earth to the moon. And we produced the same volume of data again in 2014. If, in a single year, we produced as much data as had ever been produced in the 574 years since Gutenberg's first printing press, it's clear that the overwhelming majority of all data produced has been produced in the past few years. The graph is only going to become ever-more asymptotic.

Data is getting bigger everywhere, in every aspect of our lives. Cars produce and record details about every trip you take, from fuel economy to average tyre pressure as speed and temperatures change. Every phone call you make generates permanent records – about your location, the person you called, for how long, what your talked about. Personal fitness devices from Apple Watches to Fitbits record every heartbeat, as well as exercise and sleep patterns, and then give you a nudge when you haven't been for a run for a few days or been mindful for a few hours. And conversations on social media reveal what people think – perhaps particularly vocal people in the early days of social, but today much closer to representative samples – about products, brands, personalities, and politicians.

The pace with which data is growing shows no signs of slowing down – if anything, it's accelerating – and there are two interrelated factors to support this assertion (a bit of data-driven storytelling, if you will). One is that Moore's Law of exponential growth continues apace. Gordon Moore, who cofounded two pioneering silicon chip businesses in the 1960s – Fairchild Semiconductor and Intel – observed in a seminal paper in 1965 that the number of transistors on dense, integrated circuits doubles every year or so. By 1975, Moore revised this down to every two years. What we've seen on average since 1965 is in fact a doubling about every 18 months.

Twice as many transistors in the same space every 18 months means cheaper and faster computer chips, both memory and processing chips. They're cheaper because they take up less physical space and use less of the precious material silicon. They're faster because electrons representing the ones and zeroes of digital data processing have progressively shorter distances to travel. As a result, computers continue to get faster and cheaper and storage capacity increases. Because it doubles every 18 months, this represents exponential growth according to a geometric rather than an arithmetic progression.

I'm much less interested in the data privacy or security or Big Brother aspects of the Big Data revolution. That's not to say these aren't important issues for the world to consider and agree on; they are. It's just that there are plenty of people and resources more knowledgeable about those areas than me. I'm interested in the potential that the explosion of data offers for better, fact-based, evidence-driven storytelling. This is because spotting insights and patterns and trends in data is one of the keys to better storytelling – storytelling that's rooted in human truths we couldn't record or observe or report on before, but that are now little more than a few clicks away for even entry-level users.

The second factor supporting the assertion that the Big Data revolution shows no sign of slowing down concerns the tools developed to harness, manage, and make sense of data. Just as there's more data available about almost everything that's going on in the world, so the tools for analysing and visualising Bigger Data sets are getting better and simpler and more straightforward to use. Tools like IBM Watson. Tools like Tableau. Tools like Brandwatch.

The real challenge of Big Data for storytellers is finding and isolating that little corner of it – Little Big Data, or maybe little big data – that's relevant to the story you want to tell. And then analysing it and extracting meaning from it. But the real power of using relevant, little big data sets as the foundation for better storytelling is that it's true. This is a theme that I and my co-presenters Neville Hobson and Thomas Stoeckle return to in every episode of our Small Data Forum podcast (see www.small dataforum.com or iTunes).

As I'll explore in the last chapter of this book, my contention is that we don't live in a post-truth era, whatever the Goves and Trumps and Bannons of this world would have you believe. We live in a more open and data-rich world in which anyone can cross-check what anyone else says. And for brands and corporations, politicians and personalities looking to grow and sustain loyal audiences – audiences who can become, through social media, their very advocates – truth and authenticity have never been more important.

THE POWER AND IMPACT OF STORYTELLING

As cognitive creatures, humans are hardwired to respond to stories and story structure. Stories are how we make sense of and navigate the world. We pay attention to stories, we are persuaded by stories, and we react to them. To do something different, or to carry on doing the same thing our families have been doing for generations. In March 2017, the English sociologist and broadcaster Tom Shakespeare quoted novelist Philip Pullman to Radio 4's *The Power and Peril of Stories*: "After nourishment, shelter and companionship, stories are the things we need most in the world."

Story structure was first identified – or at least first codified – by Ancient Greek philosopher Aristotle in his elegantly brief, fourth-century BC work, *The Poetics*. Considering the art forms of the day – principally epic poetry, tragedy, and comedy – he showed that people respond best to stories with a three-act structure; a beginning, a middle, and an end; a thesis (proposition), an antithesis (an opposing view or plot), and a synthesis (a bringing together). Academics and practitioners since have developed this beguilingly simple structure, labelling the first act the set-up, the second act the confrontation, and the third act the resolution. Indeed, Hollywood scriptwriters and screenwriters have also contributed much theory and practice to our understanding of story structure.

American scholar Joseph Campbell identified a 12-stage narrative pattern which he called the hero's journey and is the narrative structure many epic stories of trial and redemption follow. Common elements include the call to adventure, meeting and being trained by a mentor, tests and trials in a world different from the world inhabited by the hero, rewards for overcoming adversity, and a return to the world where the story started. Just consider *Star Wars* and *Harry Potter*, *The Odyssey* and *The Aeneid*, *Little Red Riding Hood* and *The Very Hungry Caterpillar*. Not to mention episodes, series, and entire boxed-set narrative arcs of *The Sopranos*, *Breaking Bad*, and *Modern Family*.

The reason these stories resonate so well with us is because they are based on universal principles of storytelling. The three-, 12-, and other numbered-step models – identified and expounded by academics and practitioners from Aristotle to Robert McKee – are designed to draw out universal rules from stories that resonate. Stories about people like us who have to experience something extraordinary in order to move on with their lives. We are able to make our own decisions in our much more mundane, slower-paced lives by reference to those stories that chime best with us. We may not be a king or a queen, we may not be dealing with murderous plots of evil dictators, but the power of great story, well told, is our ability to learn from it because it feels authentic and like something we *could* go through. Our lives are all reflected through the prism of *Game of Thrones*.

The literature goes on to suggest that we respond best to stories that are based on reality which itself depends on experience and evidence: stories that are rooted in genuine, data-driven insights that explain an aspect of the human condition and are wrapped in a veneer of emotion. As it is my intention to demonstrate in this book – through both theory and practice – modern-day organisational storytellers need to use data, facts, and evidence as the foundation of their stories. Not instead of stories or as the stories themselves.

The economist Steve Levitt and the journalist Stephen Dubner have proved themselves to be the masters of data-driven storytelling through their Freakonomics franchise – the books, the (partially sanctioned) film, and the podcast. At time of writing, Freakonomics Radio had just published its 300th weekly episode. *Think Like a Freak* is the closest thing they've come to writing an instructional manual, and it distils their learnings into a very readable how-to guide. They conclude this book with the line: "Stories stick with us; they move us; they persuade us to consider the constancy and frailties of the human experience."

WE'RE ALL STORYTELLERS NOW

Before the Big Data and social media revolutions, communication was a closed shop and a restricted discipline. In corporations and governments, in the private and the public sector, communication was done by communications professionals – an ironic soubriquet, given that both communications departments and communications agencies are populated by amateur generalists. Most often, these people were arts graduates, except in unusual cases that required specialist technical or biomedical knowledge, such as science or law or medicine.

Communication was a mediated monologue, with communications departments and/or agencies issuing statements, and media outlets using that information to report on what the organization did and said. They didn't blindly report, copy-and-paste style, what the PR teams put out. Not all the time, at any rate. For investigative journalism has a rich history, from Watergate to News International's phone hacking; from Woodward and Bernstein to Nick Davies. But very few individuals – particularly in listed businesses or positions of public authority and power – were mandated or even allowed to speak.

How different the world is today. Not only do most people who work in any category of organisation have personal social media profiles on which they share details of their lives outside the office (Twitter, Facebook, YouTube, Instagram), but many also use these channels and others besides (personal or company blogs, LinkedIn, Reddit) to comment and share their opinions on issues of direct relevance to the businesses they represent. They are involved in a process of impressionistic or pointillist corporate image building, adding their opinion to that of colleagues and competitors.

Today, many more voices matter. Anyone with a smartphone and a Wi-Fi connection has as much right and as much chance of being heard as anyone else. They have a chance to get their voice out there, the same chance as anyone else on social media sites – bar celebrities and high-profile commentators to whom a different set of rules apply. Only ten years ago, that would not have been possible. Influential bloggers start trends, celebrity chefs cause products or ingredients to sell out, and doctors – particularly in the U.S. – can lead unsafe drugs to be recalled from the market by regulatory authorities.

In this world – and it's a world that's not going away or slowing down any time soon – everyone in an organisation has the potential to be a storyteller. For themselves in the context of their employment, of course – such as when experts in a business attend conferences. But also on behalf of the organisation they work for. Again, for the purposes of this book, I'm less interested in the ethical or governance issues raised by the democratisation of corporate and brand storytelling. That's a matter for legal teams and counsel inside organisations, and there are plenty of good resources about how to get your employees to be a social media asset and not a liability, starting with "don't tweet drunk". What I'm keen to explore is how, given the reality of a world in which many more voices matter, we can all make better use of data and statistics to tell better, more convincing, more impactful stories.

TELLING STORIES WITH DATA AND STATISTICS

However specialised workers in the knowledge economy become – as researchers, managers, or technicians; as scientists, data analysts, or consultants – there truly are today two core skills everyone needs: analytics and storytelling. The higher up an organisation we go, the further we're likely to get from the raw data itself. But to tell stories authentically and with impact, we need to understand not just what the data show but also why and how. This is the sense in which everyone's jobs are becoming increasingly similar.

So, this book is designed to help many different people in many different types of organisation in their quest to become better, data-driven storytellers.

They might work in a communications agency – advertising, PR, or digital – and need to create a new idea for their client's product, brand, or service; for a company, an NGO, or a charity. This is the world I know best, but narrative by numbers isn't just about communications agencies. It's about communications for and by everyone.

They might have discovered something through empirical, academic, or market research and want to share what they've found out with others, to get them to see the world from their point of view, and to share the real-world impact of their discovery.

They might need to motivate others to do something differently from how they do it today. To start doing something (take up exercise, say). To stop doing something (smoking). To do more (eating fruit and veg) or less (drinking alcohol) of something. Or to do something for the first time and adopt a new habit (wear a smart watch and integrate it into their lifestyle).

They might work in an organisation on a mission and want to recruit others to their cause.

They might be tendering or pitching for a new contract and need to make a compelling case for why their bid is best for the prospective client or customer.

Or they might work in an organisation and need to persuade colleagues to adopt a new strategy. To buy from a new supplier. Or to adopt a new policy.

In each one of these instances, taking an analytical and data-driven approach to storytelling will make the story better, stronger, and more impactful. It will help a wide variety of different people, in different types of organisation and at different levels of seniority, with the task of convincing people to support them. It will assist them in the "moving business".

There are plenty of excellent books and online resources and tools to enable you to choose how best to visualise the stories you tell with data. Former Googler Cole Nussbaumer-Knaflic's *Storytelling with Data: A Data Visualization Guide for Business* is one of the best, most accessible, and most practical guides to show you how to communicate data to tell a story. She shows very clearly how different types of charts or particular elements of a graphic can distract the eye or get in the way of telling an impactful, data-driven story. She uses some of the principles of storytelling at the heart of her process, and I learned a lot from reading her book. What it's all about is given away by the subtitle after the colon. You'll find it great too, and should buy it. But this book does something different.

There are also plenty of resources extolling the virtues of taking a storytelling approach to business communications – particularly the ubiquitous and frequently pernicious PowerPoint presentation – and Anthony Tasgal's *Storytelling Book* is one of the most instructive here. If you can get past his love of the pun – something I share with him, so it didn't hold me up – there are 24 great tips that will help you "find the golden thread in your presentations". I learned a lot from reading his book, as I'm sure you will too. I've also enjoyed hearing him speak at Market Research Society events, though I think in person he slightly overdoes the argument that storytelling needs to move away from numbers and back to story, but different points of view are healthy. Add his book to your Amazon order. But again, this book does something different.

Technology, data, and the fact that many more people fulfil the role of storyteller than ten or even five years ago doesn't necessarily mean everyone does it well. The ability to look at, interrogate, and understand data sets, and then to extract only those elements of the data that you need to tell a convincing and compelling story – that takes real skill. Colleagues and bosses and clients don't necessarily need to know how you got there or to see your workings out. In fact, this is usually a distraction or irritant at best, but can be confusing and undermining to the point you're trying to make at worst. It can, indeed, be counter-productive.

This book sets out a series of five simple rules that will empower and enable any storyteller in any organisation tell better, data-driven stories no matter whom they need to convince. By sharing the pitfalls and the pratfalls I've suffered over nearly 30 years advising companies on how to tell better stories, my aim is to help the current and future generations of data-driven storytellers do their job brilliantly. And remember, we're all storytellers now.

We'll see how you can keep your storytelling simple. How to find and use only relevant data, detecting genuine signals from the siren call of noise and avoiding false positives and spurious correlations. We'll learn to beware the Curse of Knowledge and drive genuine engagement in data-driven storytelling through a combination of energy, empathy, and emotion. Data-driven storytelling is very definitely NOT all about facts, facts, facts. It's much more about knowing your audience – understanding whom you're trying to convince to do what – and then talking human. Even though companies are abstract concepts without the power of speech, it's terrifying how un-human corporate-speak can be, even though it has to be uttered or written by a person.

There. If you were in a hurry, those last two paragraphs have covered what we're going to go through in detail over the coming chapters. We'll look at each of these rules, in theory and in practice. What's more, each chapter will present a practical exercise to bring different elements of data-driven storytelling to life. Each chapter also features an example of a truly great data-driven story that has lived in the public domain, and we'll analyse what it was about these stories' use of data that made them work so well.

As legendary screenwriting coach Robert McKee is fond of saying, "a business leader should think like an author about their brand." As we'll see in the pages to follow, this is particularly true when an organisation is using data and statistics to inform their narrative and shape their storytelling.

I trust you're up for the ride.

SUMMING UP

David Ogilvy's assertion that physics was bad if Lord Rutherford couldn't explain it to a barmaid is outdated, and in the twenty-teens we'd say "member of bar staff", though hopefully not "waitron". But the principle is spot on. Everything is explicable.

Analytics and storytelling are the two core skills for most people working in the knowledge economy.

Educational systems and theory around the world have pigeon-holed people as "artists" or "scientists". This has been unhelpful.

Psychology should also shoulder some of the blame in keeping analytics and storytelling apart, particularly the caricature of the left brain/right brain dichotomy.

People like simple, single-factor explanations of phenomena, but the world is often more nuanced than that.

The exponential growth in data means we have never had more opportunity to use information as the basis for observations and ultimately insights that reveal deep human truths as the foundation of our storytelling.

The growth in the availability of data has been mirrored by the number of tools – often free – to crunch enormous volumes of data into much more manageable summaries from which narratives can be developed.

As creatures, humans are hardwired to respond to stories and story structure. It's how we make sense of the world. This was first observed by Aristotle in his *Poetics*, 2,400 years ago, but the principles of the three-act structure are eternal and eternally appealing, including as the underpinning of Hollywood screenplays, short stories, novels, and multi-series TV epics.

The rise in data has been paralleled by the explosion in social media, which has provided many more individuals in all kinds of organisations with the potential to speak as and on behalf of their employers. Today, many more voices matter.

Telling stories with data and statistics is relevant right across the knowledge economy – public and private sector, profit-making and not-for-profit.

While there are plenty of books that talk about data visualisation or storytelling, there's nothing that brings these two disciplines together – until now, and until this book.

GIVE IT A GO: THE FIVE "WHYS?"

When someone presents you with a set of data or a data-rich presentation, become a four-year-old again. Ask "Why?" whenever they draw a conclusion from data. And then ask "Why?" again. Spice it up and vary it by asking "For what purpose?" And if you work for the Royal Shakespeare Company, you could even sprinkle in the odd "Wherefore?" Do this five times on a single argument a colleague is trying to make using a key data point, a killer stat, or a critical finding from their research or data set.

It may be best let them know that you're doing this because you want to get to the bottom of whether the data really does matter – really does tell a transformational story. Because if they don't know what you're up to, they might – just might – get annoyed with you.

Build this technique into your repertoire of enquiry and interrogation whenever data is presented. It'll sort the spurious correlations from the organisation-changing data sets.

DATA-DRIVEN STORIES

How 20 years have flown (easyJet)

What's the organisation? easyJet
What's the brand? easyJet corporate and consumer brand
What's the campaign? How 20 years have flown
What's the story? In just 20 years, easyJet has gone from the bargain-bucket, no-frills airline challenger brand – from the stable of easyThis, easyThat, and easyTheOther companies from Stelios Haji-Ioannou – to the largest single carrier out of Gatwick. The company wanted to celebrate this history with its customers and show how they've grown alongside the airline, as well as use the anniversary to introduce a series of very direct offers.
How did data drive the story? easyJet aggregated data from its customers' journeys at both a macro level (to demonstrate its impact on short-haul travel) and at a personal level (to celebrate and remember journeys individual passengers had taken together).
What was the outcome of the campaign? Fourteen-fold increased response to usual email campaigns, with 7.5% of customers booking flights within 30 days of receiving tailored, personalised emails.

The fact that an organisation has been in existence for a round number of years is generally of little interest to anyone outside of the organisation itself. It can even be hard to drum up interest inside the organisation without raising yawns or suspicions among the troops that the generals are trying to divert their attention from something important by banging on about an anniversary. "Are they looking to celebrate 50 years and then make half of my team redundant while we're hanging out the corporate bunting?"

When Sir Stelios Haji-Ioannou founded easyJet in 1995, budget airlines were benefitting from EU deregulation and piling 'em high and selling 'em cheap – seats, that is. Budget airlines became a byword for value, commoditising what had been an overregulated closed shop and opening up opportunities for new entrants to the new market.

Over the following 20 years, easyJet grew to become one of the dominant carriers in continental Europe, a true short-haul success story. As it grew, its passengers grew with it. Their lives developed, their friends' and family's children's lives developed. They used easyJet to go to more and different destinations, driven by availability of routes, fashion, and consumer demand.

More and more easyJet flyers who went on holiday with the company also chose to fly orange and white on short-haul business. With the exception of a couple of destinations – and I speak with bitter experience of assuming Milan Malpensa was near Milan – easyJet secured good routes to popular destinations and started to clean up.

Management and ownership both changed and grew up, and under the leadership of Carolyn McCall from 2010 to 2017, easyJet became the largest single carrier out of Gatwick. It has also become synonymous with effective, cost-efficient, short-haul travel between the U.K. and continental Europe. And even a little beyond.

So, when easyJet turned 20, it decided it was going to use all of the data it had gathered and kept safe about its passengers over the previous two decades and build a comprehensive, integrated, multi-channel communications campaign to celebrate "How 20 years had flown". What is particularly inspiring about this example is the way that easyJet used its data to build data-driven stories that are driven by the emotion of travel – family holidays, reunions, landmark birthdays and anniversaries – and at the same time build stronger relationships between the company and its customers through their shared history. Individuals had got engaged in Dubrovnik, and easyJet had flown them there and back. What's more, as the data is about who flew where, it feels very much more like narrative from the opening scene, qualitative and quantitative though it is. Fundamentally, it's about everyone's individual hero's journeys.

Aggregated at a company level, the data was used to fuel and inform communications to celebrate the company's twentieth anniversary – in a brilliantly shot TV advert of an ever-changing family through 20 years; in press ads; on the easyJet website; and in digital banner advertising.

Where the campaign used data-driven storytelling to score a spectacular home run was in the way that relationships between easyJet and individual customers were celebrated in tailored emails celebrating the journeys they had taken together. The emails included such personal data as: destinations visited and the dates they were visited; the cumulative number of miles flown together; total number of trips made; where the traveller chose to sit most often (aisle, window, middle seats); first and last trips together; and so on.

These emails – all 12.5m of them to active members of the easyJet database – were opened 100% more than average easyJet email newsletters and saw 25% higher click-through rates than normal. Hundreds of thousands of customers liked the campaign so much that they took to social media to share easyJet's clever, thoughtful, emotional, and bespoke mechanic with their followers.

Across all markets where the campaign ran, 7.5% of customers went on to book new flights with easyJet in the next 30 days. Compared with other promotional emails sent during the same period, the personalised, emotional story of the past 20 years together proved to be more than 14 times as effective. The campaign won *Marketing*'s data creativity award in the 2016 New Thinking Awards.

As personalisation becomes both more possible and more prevalent, there is keen debate in the marketing communications community about whether it is welcomed by consumers or whether it feels a little creepy and stalkerish. For Millennials – that much-maligned, much overused demographic; let's just say "for under-35s" for the purposes of this debate – there's little problem with highly personalised content. They welcome it. It makes them feel special and cared for by the organisations who use data in this way. By contrast, there's some evidence that for older consumers, personalisation freaks them out and makes them feel like Big Brother is watching them.

For this easyJet campaign, there was very little evidence of any overt rejection of the personalisation from any demographic. Far from it. Bookings were up in response to the personalised email across the age groups, and customers of all generations took to social media to celebrate the attention the airline had showed them personally.

> *Key takeaway*: Retaining and managing personal customer data enables an organisation to aggregate that information at a global level and also make it intensely personal – and emotional – at an individual level, providing the fuel for engaging, impactful, data-driven storytelling.

NOTE

1 Edna Andrews (2014) *Neuroscience and Multilingualism*, 3.2, p. 73. Cambridge University Press. http://bit.ly/2oPH7V3

2

KEEP IT SIMPLE

Don't make it too hard for people to discern your narrative. Communicate a clear and consistent story, and offer data points over time that demonstrate progress towards your vision.

Steve Girsky, Chairman of General Motors,
Harvard Business Review (August 2014)

MORE IS VERY RARELY MORE

Rhetoric is defined as "the art of effective or persuasive speaking or writing", echoing Dan Pink's contention that we're all in the "moving business". In Classical Greek and Roman times, as well as in Georgian and Victorian England, rhetoric was taught to prospective politicians and leaders. The focus of instruction for these elites often focused on form over content, and the use of compositional techniques including figures of speech, from anaphora to zeugma. Rhetoric was helpful in making the words of the privileged few sound elegant to their peers and impressive to those they governed on the rare occasions they came into contact with the masses. But as a skillset, it didn't have much to do with how to use data and statistics to make a better case.

The mediation of public and business life through the press, radio, and TV – and more recently through interactive social and digital media channels – has changed the game for organisational storytellers. They need to be prepared to both sound good and deliver the killer evidence that persuades their audience to follow them, or vote for them, or buy their new product. Increasingly, they need to be able to do this live and in real time, responding to new developments or initiatives as they happen. To sound convincing, they have to be in complete control of their material. Though it's not just what you say but how you say it. As I'll explore in Chapter 4, to drive engagement, they need to deliver arguments rooted in data and statistics with energy, emotion, and empathy.

When organisational storytellers learn of the potential impact of the data-driven approach, many find it tempting to try to blind their audience with science. Whether you're a scientist, a Government spokesperson, or the head of R&D at a cosmetics manufacturer, it's hard to resist trotting out a roll call of evidence that supports your argument.

This is a trap you should work hard to avoid

Too much data, particularly too much unfiltered data delivered out of context, is more likely to be counter-productive. Many people find data and statistics to be confusing. This is in part because they were "badly taught" maths at school and find lists of statistics intimidating. And it's in part because they believe Mark Twain's maxim about "lies, damned lies, and statistics". Politicians have been found too-often being "economical with the actualité", a condition that rogue Tory MP Alan Clarke admitted to in a parliamentary question on the sales of arms to Iraq. Know what? He lied.

What's more, as both 2016's EU referendum in the U.K. and the U.S. presidential election demonstrated, the mere production and repetition of facts is not enough to convince voters to follow a desired course of action. While data delivered with honesty, authenticity, and credibility can help to swing contentious arguments, non-facts, anti-facts, and fake news (that's lies again) can be a massive turn-off. Trouble is, it can be a turn-on when delivered with passion and gusto. With energy, emotion, and empathy for the intended audience.

When one side of an argument relies too heavily on data and statistics, it's easy for their opponents to start picking their argument apart, one statistic at a time. Or, as Michael Gove scoffed to such memorable effect on the Brexit campaign trail, "people in this country have had enough of experts". His staunchest defenders might argue he was talking about particular experts "with acronyms who have got it consistently wrong", but this is not how Gove was heard or reported or interpreted. It's worth watching on Channel 4[1] again, if you think I'm being unfair. He didn't go quite as far as Republican politician Newt Gingrich who once infamously said "feelings are just as valid as facts", but he wasn't far off. The accusation from Gove and its impact at the ballot box led *New Scientist* to suggest, just a week after the EU referendum: "Trying to change someone's mind by giving them the facts usually just makes them dig in. For reason to triumph, scientists need to learn to engage with emotion" – an argument we'll return to in Chapter 4.

The fundamental problem is that facts are not, inherently, memorable. If you're reporting polling or attitudinal data – about who intends to vote for which politician, or which new flavour of yoghurt is liked better by toddlers versus teens – you're likely as not reporting a long list of percentages. And as brothers Chip and Dan Heath said memorably in their book *Made to Stick: Why Some Ideas Survive & Others Die*: "After a presentation, 63% of attendees remember stories. Only 5% remember statistics." Had the EU referendum come out the other way, one of the statistics that would have been both memorable and negatively impactful was the overzealous, unsupportable "We send the EU £350m a week – let's fund our NHS instead". A factoid that Brexit cheerleader Nigel Farage was already disowning on breakfast TV on 24 June 2016, when the ballot papers were still warm.

THE KIND OF STATS THAT WORK HARDEST

Ironically, indeed, the Vote Leave campaign's £350m a week statistic bears many of the hallmarks of the type of number – the type of core campaign statistic – that works hardest in data-driven storytelling. Whatever its veracity, whether anyone in the Vote Leave camp ever really pressure-tested it as a number that they would really be in a position to redirect from funding the EU to funding the NHS, the £350m figure does carry with it many of the criteria of a statistic with legs.

It's simple

The figure is clear, it ends in a zero, it doesn't include any decimal points or fractions. It's an undemanding presence that doesn't require much effort to remember it. This makes it easily repeatable and so easily transmissible. It has – in Susan Blackmore's terms – memetic potential.

It's big

Most people don't have a concept of what it would be like to have a figure this large at their personal disposal. Several times bigger than even the biggest Euromillions Lottery win in history – itself an almost unimaginable amount of money – it's clearly the kind of sum that a government could do a lot with. Government is big and spending on citizens costs money at scale, so £350m – and that amount each week – could clearly achieve something. What's more, for those liable to be opposed to spending on the EU, it becomes an instant rallying cry against the body because it's perceived to be such a waste.

It doesn't show its workings out

The number £350m has clearly been rounded – up or down, it doesn't matter which – but it's not so suspiciously round as to be unbelievable or too obviously made-up. £400m would be more suspicious, and £500m/ half a billion would feel too much like a figure plucked from the aether. But £350m feels much more like a number that has been worked on, but doesn't demand too much of the audience or require them to come on the mathematical journey. It doesn't show its workings out, but by its nature it feels like it has been worked out.

Some storytellers feel the need to give incredibly accurate numbers – sometimes to two or more decimal places – in order to show that they haven't just made the numbers up. This is particularly irritating and unnecessary in the reporting of percentages – "99.82% of Iraqis voted for Saddam". The trouble with being (too) accurate is that this starts to involve the audience into the process of calculation, and any set of figures that draws those listening into the process of calculation starts to feel like a maths lesson. ***Work hard to avoid this***. Stories that give too many numbers and show too much working out don't feel like stories. As Cole Nussbaumer-Knaflic says[2] in the narrative structure chapter of her "data visualization guide for business professionals": "A collection of numbers and words on a given topic without structure to organize them and give them meaning is useless."

It's worth saying that, although you should avoid volunteering your workings out as part of the core thrust of your storytelling, you should be able to produce them – immediately – if you're challenged to do so by a journalist or an opponent or a client. If the data or statistics pique your audience's interest sufficiently for them to ask a follow-up question or questions, fantastic. So, always keep that back of a fag packet, napkin, or spreadsheet handy just in case – joy of joys – your data-driven storytelling is so impactful that it stimulates further questions. Make that your goal in selecting the best statistics to start with, but don't be surprised if further questions are the exception, not the rule.

In storytelling, it's much better to stimulate intrigue and questions, rather than indulge in a lengthy bout of exposition and backstory without being invited to do so. As with good films and novels, so too with corporate and brand storytelling.

It's a compound variable

Wherever possible, numbers and statistics that summarise stories should pull together many different elements of calculation into a single value, again without showing the working out. It's fine to reference the fact that several different elements or line items were included in the calculation, but there's no need to walk the audience through what those calculations actually were.

Voters in the EU Referendum were aware that member state funding is a complex equation. Remainers would point to a system of rebates which meant that net contributions were very much less than the headline membership figure: that the EU invested a huge amount in projects across the U.K. which made the actual cost of membership very much less than the dues. Brexiteers could have taken the same approach and shown a balance sheet of spend versus return, and perhaps mocked the projects that saw a return because they were pointless or wouldn't have been necessary if the money had been targeted at the problem without having to be filtered via the EU. But instead, they chose to simplify all of the inputs and outputs into a single figure of almost unimaginable proportions, and a figure that represents *weekly*, not annual, contribution.

It's understandable

Indeed, the focus on £350m *a week* does a much more powerful job than aggregating the figure up to an annual total. £350m * 52 = £18bn (rounded down, naturally). Imagine the arguments in the Vote Leave camp. "We sent £18bn a year to the EU – that's an unimaginably large number – we should shout that from the rooftops, spatter that on our battle buses. Whaddayasay, Boris?" But the sheer size of the £18bn number makes it unusable or at least much less effective as a number on which to base a data-driven campaign. Not to mention – as we'll see below – that, at best, this figure represents gross, not net, contributions.

When numbers get too big, they lose meaning. While a million of anything is hard to understand, a billion of anything is much harder to grasp. The fact that total U.K. government expenditure[3] was almost £750bn in 2014–15 is hard to grasp. What that figure ends up meaning is little more than "it costs £750bn to run the U.K. each year". It's a number so far outside most people's grasp or comprehension that it just becomes a circular definition.

It's repeated ad nauseam and becomes an earworm

Peter Mandelson and Tony Blair made the Labour Party electable for the first time in nearly two decades in 1997 through a number of highly effective strategies. They dragged the party to the right (or the centre, depending on your starting point). This involved them repositioning the party as "new Labour", mitigating Middle Englanders' concerns that a Labour

1 **cut class sizes for 5, 6 and 7 year-olds**
by using money saved from the assisted places scheme.

2 **cut NHS waiting lists by treating an extra 100,000 patients** as
a first step by releasing £100 million saved from NHS red tape

3 **get 250,000 under-25 year-olds off benefit and into work** by
using money from a windfall levy on the privatised utilities

4 **fast track punishment for persistent young offenders** by
halving the time from arrest to sentencing

5 **legislate for a Scottish Parliament in our first year** by holding a
referendum on devolution and campaigning for a **yes** vote

Published by E Smith, 56 Tuphall Road, Hamilton ML3 6TB.
Printed by Superquickprint, 23/31 Castle Street, Hamilton ML3 6BU.

Figure 2.1 The 1997 new Labour election pledge card, Scottish Labour version

government would mean industrial action paralysing public services and
the PM huddling with the TUC over beer and sandwiches at Number 10.
They also successfully reassured the British public that new Labour could
be trusted running the economy. One of the most effective arrows in their
quiver was incredibly simple, direct, and of course data-driven.

What Peter and Tony also did incredibly effectively ahead of the 1997
election campaign was agree on the six core areas where new Labour
would make a difference. These were captured in a simple, straightforward pledge card. The pledge cards were wallet-sized and issued to all
party members and campaign activists. They represented the summary of
new Labour's costed pledges for what it planned to do when it got into
office. Each one of the pledges had numbers and statistics and targets
attached to them – something that came back to haunt the party when
in office.

All activists – whether on the doorstep or appearing on BBC TV's
Question Time – were expected and required to focus on the six areas. All
were required to learn, know, and follow-up each pledge with the data
and statistics that supported them, particularly as prospective voters or
TV interviews showed some interest or challenge for any specific pledge.
What the pledge card did was serve as a summary and a bridge and a
jumping-off point for debate on the issues where new Labour felt safe and
confident its policies would make a significant difference.

What new Labour created in the pledge card was a classic executive summary of a data-driven storytelling campaign, and the party foot soldiers deployed this weapon as intended and directed. It meant that the campaign stayed very much on-message. As an analogue piece of card in the wallet, it was less sinister and apparently controlling than pagers sharing soundbites and slogans, an early use of political tech that was used as a stick to beat new Labour once it took power. What the card ensured was that new Labour talked with one voice, dominated the debate on its terms, and won the first of two landslides, the first of three elections. The stuff of the Corbynistas' wildest dreams.

The 1997 pledge card made new Labour's pledges become a close-knit set of earworms. A general election is rarely about a single issue – whatever Theresa May's declared motivation in calling the 2017 snap election – and this contrasts with referenda. While referenda in general – and the EU Referendum in particular – are about more than single issues, they do require voters to vote on a single question. Where the Brexiteers were so successful with their relentless focus on the "£350m a week" killer statistic is that they repeated it, *ad nauseam*, until it, too, became an earworm. The defining earworm and statistic of the campaign. When Remainers looked to rubbish or discredit it, they referenced it. It became shorthand for cost and value of EU membership. It was created and owned and championed by the winning side, even if they disowned and dropped it less than four hours after the result was confirmed. But that didn't matter. By then, it had done its job.

It avoids the inconvenient truth of context

Sometimes, context is invaluable in data-driven storytelling. Setting data and statistics in their proper context can show how one course of action can have impact outside the immediate frame of reference. It's more honest, holistic, and even-handed and shows that the storyteller has considered the issue in the round, rather than just from their own point of view. We'll come back to empathy in Chapter 4.

At other times, avoiding context – hiding the full picture from the audience – can make the data and statistics chosen by the storyteller perform much more powerfully. This is exactly what the Vote Leave campaign did with the £350m figure, cunningly derived from the Government's own data and based on gross and not net spend after rebates. They used a round (but not too suspiciously round), big (but not too big) figure to make their case. What they didn't do or use or consider was the money the U.K. got back from the EU in the form of investment or rebates, agricultural, industrial, or regenerative. Nor did they choose to present what net expenditure meant in terms of overall Government expenditure.

The totality of U.K. Government expenditure after rebates and subsidies provided by the EU offer up the context that Vote Leave was so keen to omit. The official data show that the net cost of the U.K.'s membership of the EU for 2015 was the still impressively big figure of £3.7bn. But set in context, £3.7bn represents half of one percent. In statistical terms, 0.5% is a rounding error. A figure so vanishingly small as to be of no statistical or practical significance.

Let's look at it another way. In psychological and medical trials, an experiment is not deemed to have been caused by anything other than chance if it doesn't have a probability (or p) value of less than 5%. Convention has it that this is often written as $p < 0.05$. What this means is that, if we'd conducted the same experiment 100 times, we would have got a different outcome in fewer than five of the experiments. Flip that on its head and we see that, for every 20 times we did run the manipulation, it would come out differently in less than one experiment. And for psychologists, this means they're pretty confident they've found something interesting; the manipulation achieved something of interest that is very unlikely to have happened by chance. In some medical experiments, the probability threshold is set twice as high, at $p < 0.10$.

If psychology is prepared to accept probability values ten times as large as the Brexiteers are prepared to invest in the EU – and medicine 20 times as large – this tells us that Vote Leave was street smart (if deceitful) not to put the true value of expenditure in its proper context.

Here's another analogy. Let's scale it down to salaries or mortgage payments. If you're used to taking home £2,500 per month and one month

VARIABLE	VALUE
£3.7bn: cost of EU membership after rebates	£3,700,000,000
£735bn: all UK Government spending	£735,000,000,000

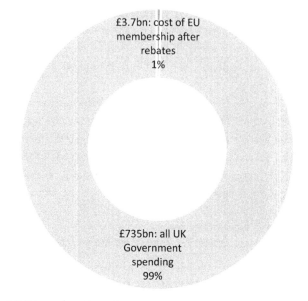

£3.7bn: cost of EU
membership after
rebates
1%

£735bn: all UK
Government
spending
99%

Figure 2.2 EU membership cost

Cost of EU membership after rebates in the context of all U.K. Government spending: £3.7bn out of £735bn (2014–15)

Source: U.K. Government's Public Expenditure Statistical Analyses for 2015

URL: www.gov.uk/government/statistics/public-expenditure-statistical-analyses-2015

your pay packet shows you're being paid £2,487.50. Would you quibble? Would you notice? Or imagine your direct debit for mortgage payments is £1,250 per month and one month your mortgagor takes £1,256.25. Again, would you notice? Would it be worth raising?

That's the scale of the cost of EU membership to the U.K. as a percentage of annual expenditure. If those numbers had been presented, the result might have been rather different – if the population at large had seen EU expenditure in its proper context. As it was, the Remain camp decided to embark on Project Fear and use literally incredible scare stories about what could happen to industrial output and jobs and tax receipts, and their over-reliance on too much fact presented in too much detail ran their campaign into the buffers. Thanks, Gideon and Dave. A poor, data-stuffed campaign was run by pushing statistic after statistic on a confused public with little emotional wrapping other than fear and dread.

The zombie status of "£350m a week"

Since its first, extensive outing during the EU Referendum campaign, £350m a week has taken on the status of a zombie statistic, one that refuses to die no matter how many credible, authoritative commentators try to kill it off. Independent analysts – including Government statisticians – have pawed over the statistic and its data sources and sought to discredit it. Three major points of contention have been its total lack of context, the fact that it ignores rebates and subsidies, and whether the carefully worded slogan on Boris' battle bus implied a post-Brexit settlement would ever use the money "saved" to go directly to the NHS.

And just when it was thought that the victorious Brexit camp had wrung all that they could from it, Foreign Secretary Johnson gave it new life by repeating the number and again suggesting it be earmarked for the NHS. In a 4,000-word extended manifesto designed to undermine a major speech from PM Theresa May to European Leaders, he said in the *Daily Telegraph*[4] on 15 September 2017:

> *And yes – once we have settled our accounts, we will take back control of roughly £350 million per week. It would be a fine thing, as many of us have pointed out, if a lot of that money went on the NHS, provided we use that cash injection to modernise and make the most of new technology.*

This led Sir David Norgrove, Head of the U.K. Statistics Authority, to rebuke Johnson for confusing gross and net contributions and in so doing wilfully misleading the British public for a second time. A proper telling off and rap over the knuckles. Though I doubt it's the last time BoJo will wheel out his favourite pet zombie.

UK Statistics Authority	Telephone:	0207 592 8645
1 Drummond Gate	E-mail:	david.norgrove@statistics.gsi.gov.uk
London	**Website:**	**www.statisticsauthority.gov.uk**
SW1V 2QQ		

Chair of the UK Statistics Authority, Sir David Norgrove

Rt Hon Boris Johnson MP
Foreign Secretary
Foreign and Commonwealth Office
King Charles Street
London
SW1A 2AH

17 September 2017

Dear Foreign Secretary,

I am surprised and disappointed that you have chosen to repeat the figure of £350 million per week, in connection with the amount that might be available for extra public spending when we leave the European Union.

This confuses gross and net contributions.[1] It also assumes that payments currently made to the UK by the EU, including for example for the support of agriculture and scientific research, will not be paid by the UK government when we leave.

It is a clear misuse of official statistics.

Yours sincerely

Sir David Norgrove

Figure 2.3 Letter from Sir David Norgrove to Boris Johnson

CHOOSING THE KILLER STATISTIC

There are other criteria you can use to make sure you choose the perfect killer statistic. Data that can show trends – particularly trends that can project reliably into the future – are helpful. Done right and in a way that does, in the end, accurately predict the future, predictive analytics can be incredibly powerful.

The trouble here is that those in the prediction business generally have a very poor track record in accurately and reliably predicting the future, whether they're stock market analysts, bookmakers, weather forecasters, or astrologers. They might get on a lucky roll and predict winners or weather right four or five times in a row. But the roll won't carry on forever. The statistical law of regression to the mean will interfere and bring outcomes back to the average of what might be expected, and future-gazers' models will be found lacking because they haven't considered enough input variables in building their model. They'll rely too heavily on cognitive heuristics or shortcuts that enable them to cope with huge volumes of data quickly but not necessarily effectively, making their incorrect predictions predictably incorrect. Daniel Kahneman's *Thinking, Fast and Slow* explains how and why in detail, and for the truly committed, it's worth going back to Kahneman and Tversky's original papers.

And so, in summary, for its simplicity, its bigness (but not too-bigness), the omission of workings-out, the fact that it brought several data points together and was understandable, its earworm qualities, and the judicious decision not to set it in context . . . for all these reasons, Vote Leave's "£350m to the NHS" truly was an inspired example of data-driven storytelling, however flawed or dishonest or downright wrong it was and I and the rest of the 48% may know it to have been. Remoaners, eh? Such sore losers.

BE SIMPLEST OF ALL IN YOUR LANGUAGE

So far in this chapter, we have considered the different criteria you should use when choosing the right data and the best statistics to tell your story. At the heart of what we've covered so far is the need to be simple, clear, and understandable. While complex mathematical and statistical techniques and processes need to be applied to numbers to build a rigorous, evidence-based story, these need to be stripped back and hidden away when it comes actually to telling the story. Just as important as the numbers chosen to make your point are the words you use to tell the story.

When physicist Richard Feynman was awarded the Nobel Prize for Physics, he was asked if he could explain in just three minutes why he'd won the prize. In a rare misstep, Feynman is reputed to have answered: "If I could explain it in three minutes, it wouldn't have won the Nobel Prize." With all due respect, Dr Feynman, you're wrong. Anything can be explained top line – in an elevator pitch – in three minutes. It should be possible to explain it in a sentence and ideally in a phrase. $e = mc^2$, anyone?

It's always possible to make difficult concepts easier to understand by using simpler and more straightforward language. Note: this is not about dumbing down. It's about talking human, a theme we will return to in Chapter 6. The words chosen by businesses and other organisations are very often far too complex and difficult to understand. Sometimes that's to do with jargon (and we'll come back to that, too). But more often it comes down to an overly complex writing style. As soon as they're given the scope to write on behalf of or in the voice of an organisation, normally fluent communicators default to an obscure, fuzzy, pretentious form of words that's never come out of any human's mouth.

One of the most straightforward ways in which organisational storytellers can use data to make their storytelling more compelling is in writing in a simple and straightforward way. Fortunately, there are a several different diagnostic tools that you can use to check whether your language is telling your story simply, clearly, and effectively. And suitably enough for a book about telling stories with data and statistics, all of these produce – erm – data and statistics about the words you use.

The **Gunning Fog Formula** analyses text and generates a score that's a school grade. This equates to the number of years of formal education a reader would need to have passed through to be able to understand the text with ease at first reading. The **SMOG Index** does something similar, though it also benefits from associations with London's peasouper smogs ("smoke" + "fog"), worst in the so-called Big Smoke of 1952. For five days in December, pollution plus weather made it hard to see your hand in front of your face. The analogy with smoggy, unclear writing is almost too appealing. What's more, SMOG is an acronym for Simple Measure of Gobbledygook. It, too, creates a school grade score. Other tests include the **Automated Readability Index**, the **Fry Readability Formula**, and the **Coleman–Liau Index**. There's a world of text analysis to which most people are entirely oblivious. *(Note: this paragraph scores 10.3 on the Gunning Fog, but 12.4 on the SMOG Index, as calculated using http://readable.io).*

Perhaps the simplest, most widely used, and most useful of all the tools available is the **Flesch–Kincaid 'reading ease' score**. The FK score is based simply on the number of words per sentence and the number of syllables per word. The shorter your sentences, and the fewer long words you use, the higher your score.

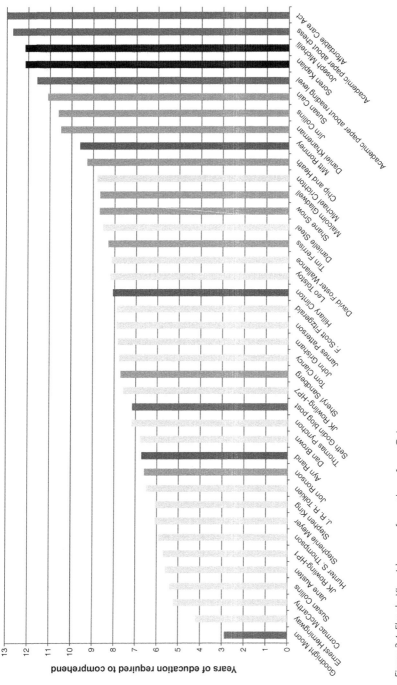

Figure 2.4 Flesch–Kincaid scores for authors from @shanesnow

FK scores typically range from 0 to 100, although there's a sentence in *Moby Dick* that scores -146.77 and one in Proust that scores -515.10. Journalist and head of *Contently*, Shane Snow,[5] produced a great study[6] of the FK scores generated by different authors and sources, which is well worth the detour. Above is a typical chart, with text analysed from children's classic *Goodnight Moon* (FK of less than 3) and the Affordable Care Act (aka Trump's favourite Obamacare) (FK 13).

As we're particularly interested in this book in how organisational storytelling is mediated through print, broadcast, and online media outlets, the following table gives typical Flesch-Kincaid scores for a variety of different channels.

The FK score is accompanied by a grade level. This represents the U.S. school grade a reader needs to have attained to be able to understand the text in question with ease. The test, scores, and grade levels are based on well-validated psychological tests. Essentially, the longer the words and the longer the sentences, the harder they are to understand; to "parse", as linguists say. Longer processing time of interminable sentences mean the start of these sentences fall out of working memory. This makes us fail to understand, lose interest, and become less engaged.

Technical topics based on scientific or medical breakthroughs are often full of technical terms. These are often polysyllabic words derived from Latin or Greek. They go on for ages. String a few of those together and soon you've got an incomprehensible sentence. Keeping language

Table 2.1 Typical Flesch Kincaid scores for different publications

Source	FK 'reading ease' score
BuzzFeed (list post)	96
Harry Potter and the Chamber of Secrets	85
Cosmopolitan magazine	78
Guardian homepage	64
The Economist	43
Apple iTunes Terms & Conditions	33
Standard insurance policy	10

simple and easy to understand drives engagement and interest. It has the same effect as an enthusiastic person talking about one of their passions in an entertaining but straightforward way.

Do this simply, clearly, authentically. Be you. If you're Eric, be very Eric. Not Jeremy or Bobby-Ann.

In our ever-more digital world, when people want to find out about your organisation, company, or brand, they look online. Whether they're about to buy from you or they just want to comment on your customer service, most people find that what you say in your own (or owned) media channels says a lot about you. About whether you deserve their loyalty or the sharp edge of their tongue.

The language you choose is a critical first step in shaping perceptions of your organisation, as it is for your competitors. Sure, it's important what influencers say in editorials, blogs, and social media, but getting people to understand what you do and why you do it really starts with the story you tell about yourself.

SUMMING UP

In this chapter, we've focused on the basics of how to tell stories with data and statistics. The advice from General Motors' Steve Girsky not to make it too hard for people to discern your narrative demands clarity and consistency.

Choosing the right data and statistics can make the difference between winning and losing – an election campaign, a sales battle with a competitor, the hearts and minds of your audience.

The always-on nature of modern media means organisational storytellers need to choose and use the right data and statistics sparingly – and be prepared to give a fuller explanation "if asked".

Don't blind you audience with science – always be selective in your choice of data and statistics.

More is very rarely more.

People respond to stories more than they do to numbers. Data and statistics should be the underpinning or the foundation of your stories, not the stories themselves.

Be simple. Avoid decimals and fractions. But don't make your numbers too suspiciously round.

Use big numbers – not too big so that you become literally incomprehensible.

Don't show your workings-out, but be prepared to share how you got to your answer – including the intricacies of your methodology and calculations – if pressed by the knowledgeable or interested.

Compound data together to create variables that summarise the meaning of your story. But be careful you don't lose important details along the way.

Tell your audience what you're going to tell them. Tell them. And then tell them what you've told them. Over and over and over again. That's the way to create a truly memorable earworm.

Use context where it helps to advance your case. But be aware of what you're hiding if you fail to set the data you choose to use in its proper context.

Be simplest of all in the language you use – short sentences and simple, short words.

Being clear is not the same as dumbing down.

GIVE IT A GO

Keep it simple, smarty-pants

The simpler the text, the easier it is to understand. The easier copy is to understand, the fewer times people need to read it before they understand it – ideally just the once. And the quicker they understand it, the quicker they can respond to it. Buy your product. Support your cause. Decide that you are the party or candidate they want to vote for.

Go to your organisation's About Us page. If you don't have an About Us page (unlikely), how about your most recent personal statement or biography. Highlight and copy the text into a new Pages or Word file and save it. Then go to one of the online readability tools available. Readability Formulas is free (www.readabilityformulas.com), and I subscribe to www.readable.io for a modest annual fee. Paste the copy into the text window and find out how simple or complex your copy is.

I favour Flesch–Kincaid, which – like many of the other tools available – is based on words per sentence and syllables per word. If your text has scored higher than you'd hoped in reading age and lower than you'd expected for readability, save a fresh copy of the text and start working on it. Make the sentences shorter. Replace long, Latinate, abstract words with short, pithy, Anglo-Saxon equivalents. Cut out all the fat. And then run the textual analysis again. You'll be surprised how quickly you can make even complex text much more readable, much more understandable, and much more likely to trigger action for your audience. Build language complexity analysis into your regular, storytelling routine.

Simples.

DATA-DRIVEN STORIES

This Girl Can

What's the organisation? Sport England, a representative body providing services and funding for sport in England
What's the brand? Women's participation in sport
What's the campaign? This Girl Can
What's the story? How data about the drags and drivers of women's participation in sport changed attitudes and behaviours.
How did data drive the story? The planning of the campaign was shaped by research among 14–60-year-old women that showed one of the principle reasons why they didn't get involved was because they were afraid of what others thought of them taking part.
What was the outcome of the campaign? An additional 1.6m U.K. women regularly taking part in sport, a sustainable and sustained increase from 2014 to 2017.

Changing attitudes and beliefs with a data-driven storytelling campaign is one thing. Changing the behaviour of millions of people is nothing short of a miracle. But it's exactly what Sport England's This Girl Can campaign achieved in less than two years.

The benefits of sport and regular exercise are well-established. To individual health and wellbeing. To mental as well as physical health. And to society at large, particularly a society beginning to be weighed down by an epidemic of obesity and inactivity, with knock-on costs already taking up scarce health service resources. Society would be better off – physically, spiritually, and financially – if more people regularly took part in sport.

The message about the long-term benefits of sport and exercise are failing to get through, despite up to 13 years of regular weekly exercise at school. Something is clearly going wrong at school age, because more than a third of the least physically active school girls agree with the statement that they feel like their body is on show in PE lessons and this makes them like PE less.

Once school's out and games cease to be compulsory, active participation in sport in England falls off dramatically. The lack of participation in sport after school age is particularly common among English women. Research commissioned by Sport England showed that 2m fewer women aged 14–60 play regular sport compared with men of the same age.

Sport England also found that more than 75% of the women not regularly playing sport say they would like to, but the research discovered that the fundamental factor holding them back is fear of being judged by others: the fear of what others will think about their physical appearance and ability when they see them exercising. A quarter said that they "hate the way I look" when taking part in sport. And – wrongly – most women believe they are alone in their fears, whereas the research pointed to this being a universal truth.

Sport England and its ad agency FCB Inferno put research, data, and statistics at the heart of their communications development and planning process. They knew they needed to produce an emotional, emotive campaign to help women understand they were not alone in their fears and anxieties and to empower them to understand the very real value – to

Figure 2.5 This Girl Can

themselves, their families, and their communities – if they did become involved in sport and exercise.

Part of the reason for the campaign's impact and success has been its use of real women, not airbrushed celebrities, in its films – real women who have overcome the anxieties that are holding back many millions of their peers across the country. By using emotive imagery and film, the campaign was able to address very real, very specific concerns that have been holding women back from active participation in sport, including the unjustified misconception that getting sweaty and red in the face is just not feminine. This misconception was held by almost half of the women surveyed by Sport England. It was overtly addressed by the two of the campaign taglines, "Sweating like a pig. Feeling like a fox" and "Damn right I look hot". And perhaps most memorably of all, at a time when women's football in the U.K. is finally coming of age, "I kick balls. Deal with it".

At every step of the creative and executional process, the campaign used data and statistics as the rational underpinning to unlock the insights that made the campaign so powerful and effective. As a result of the campaign, 1.6m more women took part in sport regularly than before it aired. What's more, the rate of change – the rate at which women are taking up sport compared with men – is now to women's advantage.

The second This Girl Can campaign broke in early 2017, focusing on older women participating in sport. Early results already suggest that it is likely to be just as impactful.

Key takeaway: Data and statistics can be used as the foundations of incredibly powerful public education campaigns that actively and sustainably change behaviour.

NOTES

1 www.youtube.com/watch?v=GGgiGtJk7MA
2 *Storytelling with Data* (Wiley), pp. 177–8.
3 www.gov.uk/government/statistics/public-expenditure-statistical-analyses-2015
4 http://bit.ly/2y8KgUa
5 https://shanesnow.contently.com
6 http://bit.ly/1L9M5P5

3

FIND AND USE ONLY
RELEVANT DATA

When we know why we do what we do, everything else falls into place.
Simon Sinek (2011), *Start with Why*

WADING THROUGH THE SMOG

The bigness of Big Data can be intimidating. Many storytellers don't know where to start in their quest to track down the relevant corner of Big Data – what I call little big data – which will prove most fruitful in building an evidence-based narrative. They can't see the forest for the trees.

I well remember the difficulties one of my data analytics teams had to overcome some years ago in building the right search strings to harvest news and social media conversations about Tide washing powder and laundry liquid. Now Tide is the number one laundry brand in the U.S., but it's also the name of a popular sports team (the Crimson Tide, an American football team from Alabama), as well as the name of a popular film of the same name as the sports team, starring Gene Hackman and Denzel Washington. Oh, and it's also the word that describes the phenomenon of the sea coming in and out, affected by the gravitational pull of the moon. Every coastal town or city in every English-speaking country in the world (and quite a lot more besides) publishes tide tables to help sailors and fishermen with their daily work. Increasingly, these are published and updated online.

Searching for Alpha Romeo, Audi, or Adobe – for Pepsi, Pampers, or Pantene – poses relatively few problems and brings back relatively few false positives (we'll come back to them later in this chapter). It's one of the reasons brand names are so distinctive and so powerful around the world. They stand out like beacons from the mass of text-rich data around them – in newspapers, on websites, in social media streams. But when a product's brand name is a common word used in other contexts – as in the case of "Tide" vs "tide" – you need to be constantly narrowing down your search. To be sure you're not bringing back a load of meaningless content that has nothing to do with your brand, you (or more likely your analysts) need to learn and become fluent in a new language: Boolean.

Boolean is the language of logic, and it allows you to search for certain terms but in the right context; within xx characters or words of the target word; always exclude if it's within yy words of a disqualifying term, and so on. Boolean is the language of AND and NOT and OR. Relatively straightforward for Tide laundry products. Not quite so easy when the number one competitor of Tide in the U.S. is (or was at the time) a brand called All. Nice, inclusive brand name. Designed to tell its users that its product has no boundaries, for its users or the clothes it can clean. And also, the thirty-sixth most common word in the English language. My mind boggles at the Boolean flips the analytics team had to do to find relevant mentions of "All" (NOT "all" AND "laundry" OR "washing" AND "clothes" etc.).

Some – mistakenly, I believe – consider the task of identifying and isolating the right data to be a technology problem. Yes, technology is important. You need a tool or a platform capable of extracting meaningful, relevant content from the smog that threatens to obscure the data you're looking for. These are the kinds of challenges that face the security services daily in looking to identify terrorists based on keywords or constantly changing code words. You might also need a tool that can spot trends and patterns, separating regularities from irregularities, and find meaning from the morass. But fundamentally, identifying the relevant corner of little big data isn't a tech problem.

START WITH "WHY?"

While technology matters, purpose matters a whole lot more. When looking to generate and distil the right data and statistics to tell your data-driven story, you need also to have identified and clearly articulated your purpose. Mr Purpose is Simon Sinek.

During the first decade of the 2000s, Sinek was a busy, successful consultant, building and growing a practice with national and international clients from a U.S. base. As the years went by, the business got bigger and the revenues grew. But Sinek became increasingly dissatisfied with and stressed out by his business. From the outside, everything was rosy; from the inside, he was torn apart. Not from the stress of the business struggling, but rather, from the stress of not knowing why he was in business in the first place.

Sinek observed that truly great businesses that have leaders and employees who want to come to work have a clearly articulated sense of purpose of why they are in business. By "Why?", Sinek doesn't mean to make money or be successful or be the best in class. Salaries and revenue and status are helpful, often very attractive by-products or benefits that follow to those who work in businesses that are successful. But the impacts of these benefits are short-lived in the hierarchy of workers' needs. Salary hikes and promotions have been found to have a positive impact on productivity for all of . . . 11 days.

In his book *Drive*, fellow American business writer Dan Pink identifies the three principle drivers of twenty-first century workplace motivation as autonomy (the freedom to make choices about how you do what you do), mastery (doing what you're good at doing), and purpose (doing something for a reason).

By "Why?", Sinek also means the types of problems and challenges the business helps to solve. He means the contribution they make to lives of the clients they serve. From Apple's original purpose – "We're here to remove the barrier of having to learn to use a computer" – to IKEA's "To create a better everyday life for the many". From the BBC's "To enrich people's lives with programmes and services that inform, educate, and entertain" to Coke's "To refresh the world . . . to inspire moments of happiness".

From Nintendo's "To put smiles on the faces of everyone we touch" to Patagonia's "Build the best product, cause no unnecessary harm, use business to inspire and implement solutions to the environmental crisis".

Purpose is much more than a corporate mission or vision statement. It's what an organisation stands for: its principles and ethos. It's an expression of the long-term journey a business is on, adding meaning to what it does. It also makes it very much more straightforward to build emotional connections into product propositions, and between employers and employees. When Dove found its purpose in challenging the stereotypes of the beauty industry (see the case study at the end of Chapter 6), global brand director Silvia Lagnado would regularly walk past scores of Unilever's brightest and best marketers on her way to her office. They had queued up because they all wanted to come and work on a brand with such a clearly defined purpose, and direct action seemed to be the way to do it.

Back to Simon Sinek. Once he'd worked out the role and importance of purpose in business, Sinek realised that his purpose was to let the world know about the transformative effect that finding and expressing your own purpose can have on your business. So, he wound up his consultancy business and pitched up at TEDxPuget Sound in September 2009 and gave his talk "How great leaders inspire action". It was here that he introduced to the global stage his now famous concentric circles, with "WHY" in the inner circle or bullseye, "HOW" in the middle circle, and "WHAT" in the outer circle.

In this talk – now the second most-watched TED Talk of all time at 35m views and counting – Sinek showed how most companies start to talk about themselves by talking about *what* they do (what, what, what, what, what). A few focus on *how* – their proprietary methodology that sets them apart. And only a very few start with *why*. Half a dozen times in 18 scant minutes, Sinek insists – with increasing urgency – "People don't buy what you do, they buy why you do it". With that talk, he established a new business and new business model and a new approach to organisational storytelling.

And so, while identifying and isolating the right data and statistics are of course technological problems, much more importantly they're philosophical challenges. And it starts with "Why?"

ASK THE RIGHT QUESTIONS

I see this challenge as more of a detective story than a fishing expedition. A task where you're working from the bottom up – from the first clues – rather than from the top down. Working from the top down – trying to cast a net over everything and only hold onto those bits of information that are relevant – is like trying to boil the ocean. You might make a very little progress in a very few areas, but you're very unlikely to find what you're looking for. If you do stumble across it, you may well not recognise that you've found it. And if you do recognise that you've found it, you're very unlikely to have the confidence that it is – after all – what you were looking for. As Big Data becomes Bigger and Bigger Data, the top-down approach will become progressively less effective.

The same is true of crafting research briefs and questionnaires, the answers from which you want to use to extract insights about those you're interviewing. Before even starting to sketch out research questions to help you better understand attitudes, motivations, and behaviours, you need to first get a thorough grounding in the topic area you're looking to understand further through the research. This doesn't mean cooking the research questions so they give you the answers you're looking for. That is only ever a game of short-term returns. Rather, it means gathering and using all the intelligence there is about the topic area to help create the best and most relevant possible hypotheses to test. And you can only do that by a proper immersion in the subject area. By being curious and asking questions and having receivers always on.

There are several powerful examples of data-driven stories that have been created in just this way through research detailed in the case studies in this book. Consider Dove's Campaign for Real Beauty and the research-driven revelation that only 2% of the world's women would describe themselves as beautiful (see pp. 122–125). Consider Sport England's This Girl Can, based in part on the finding that 85% of women feel intimidated and held back from taking part in sport or exercise for fear of what others might think about how they look or how they perform, about how they may be judged (see pp. 39–42). And consider Tesco's Producers As Heroes, and the insight derived from in-store competition entries that customers perceive the tasty, fresh produce from Britain's farms sold at Tesco as high quality; what makes a quality product is at least as much the responsibility of the producer who grew, raised, or made it as the retailer who brings it to you (see pp. 62–65).

On the face of it, market research and social media analytics are very different disciplines. Different audiences, different motivations, different modalities of communication. But increasingly, many progressive thinkers now think of social media analytics as among the purest and most spontaneous forms of market research available. Social media content is produced by an increasingly representative sample of the general population, and personal and demographic information is often attached to posts and tweets and shares. And it's viewed as spontaneous and unfiltered, because to be moved to talk about an issue or a product on one or more of your chosen social media platforms, it must have made you particularly happy or sad or angry. Indeed, although delivered through competition entries, the Tesco story below (see pp. 62–65) is a good example of data and statistics generated by an initiative that wasn't set up to deliver this kind of intelligence.

AVOID FALSE POSITIVES

For storytellers looking to use data and statistics as the foundation of their narratives, there are a couple of specific, significant challenges you need to be aware of in relation to what you think the data may be telling you. These relate to the wide availability of large amounts of data generated both by and about organisations, as well as the myriad other sets of data that are made available by both public and private sector organisations. Put simply, there's just so much data available, it can be difficult to know where to start, what to pay attention to, and what to ignore.

There are all kinds of data you and your organisation might collect that could be useful as the foundation of better, evidence-based storytelling. In almost every case, this data is more useful for storytelling if it's trended over time, to allow you to see how things are changing. Changes can arise for various reasons, including campaigns from you and your competitors or peers, new market entrants, or changes in regulation or legislation. In no particular order, the data sources an organisation has at its disposal can include:

- **News data and analysis** – What are people saying about you and your competitors and peers in the (increasingly online) news media? What kind of language do journalists use when they're talking about your category? Are they routinely more positive when they talk about you or your competitors? Are your people or your competitors' spokespeople more likely to be sought out for a point of view? What is the sentiment of the articles written? Is it positive, neutral, or negative? What methodology is used to ascribe sentiment? Is it done by computer algorithm, using – say – automated natural language processing (which often isn't much better than chance)? Or is it manually coded by real human analysts? Is all of the content scored for sentiment, or just a sample? Is that sample representative? Where in the country or the world is there more or less interest in your organisation? Who are the most influential journalists writing in the area you're involved in?
- **Social media data and analytics** – Similar to news media data (though usually much shorter form in terms of original content). What are people saying about you and your competitors and peers on social media platforms and in blogs? What pictures are they posting? What type of language do they use when they're talking about you? What's the sentiment? Who are the most influential individuals in social media as measured by how many other people they reach (number of followers etc.), how many people they stimulate to share their content (their resonance), and how much they talk about you rather than competitors or peers (their relevance)? Last time I checked, there were several hundred different social media analytics platforms, so it's hard to know where to start in terms of recommendations. Because they're generally agreed to be one of the best, because they're sons and daughters of Sussex born out of my second alma mater the University of Sussex, and because they're generous with helpful content, I'd recommend starting with Brandwatch[1]

to harvest and analyse both news and social media content, though of course this comes at a cost.

- **Sales data** – What have you sold in which locations over the relevant period? How do your sales compare between online and offline? What's a typical customer journey?
- **Market research and polling data** – What do people think about your category, your company, and its products? How do their attitudes compare with what they think about your competitors? Or about peers, or businesses you respect or aim to emulate?
- **Employee data** – How do your people feel about working for you? Do they live to work or work to live? Do they understand and can they repeat your corporate purpose and philosophy? Do they even know you have a purpose? Are they genuinely engaged? Are they coming on the same journey as you're intending to lead? How long do they stay with you? Are you experiencing excessive, industry-standard, or below-average churn?
- **Reputation data** – What do people – from specific interest groups to the general public – think about your organisation? Do you have a good reputation? How could it be improved? How are you doing compared with your competitors, peers, or benchmark companies? What are the drivers of your reputation, good or bad? Are some more readily changed than others? What do people think of the quality of leadership and vision in your organisation?
- **Market data** – What's the dynamic of the marketplace in which you operate? Are you a monopoly supplier, are there several competitors, and where do you rank? Are there new entrants or challengers entering your market? What are the opportunities for you to expand into new or adjacent markets? Is digital technology disrupting your market and are some new entrants threatening to "do an AirBnB or an Uber?"
- **Analyst reports** – What do financial analysts think and say about your performance? Are you seen as progressive or stick-in-the-mud? How do you compare with competitors and peers?

In addition to your own data, other data sets are also increasingly being made available. These data sets are usually free to download and can be incredibly useful for organisations looking to build a story based on sociodemographic trends. They include:

- **Health data** – National and transnational league tables of morbidity and mortality – sickness and deaths. The late, great Hans Rosling – perhaps the greatest data-driven storyteller on the subject of global public health, and the subject of a profile in Chapter 7 – was instrumental in securing and providing access to a wealth of health data. The Gapminder[2] site he set up, run since his untimely death by his children, is a good starting point. The World Health Organization (WHO) and national health departments, including the U.K. Department of Health, also provide good sources of data. As do the bigger, publicly funded health research projects in both the EU and the U.S., such as the Framingham Heart Study. The U.S. National Institutes of Health web resources are helpful here.

- **Wealth and income data** – How much people earn, how much they spend, and how much they owe can all help you build powerful narratives. So can data about tax revenue – individual and corporate – and the size and scale of different businesses. Data sets in the U.K. to look out for include those made available by the National Audit Office, HM Revenue & Customs, the Office of Budget Responsibility, and the Office of National Statistics. Corporate annual reports – covering everything from financial performance to sustainability – often also provide a mine of relevant information.

- **Government spend data** – The organisations listed immediately above also provide time series data of U.K. Government expenditure (and income) for different departments. Planned and phased investment in rail infrastructure, for instance, could provide the ammunition a civil engineering firm needs to make a case – and tell the story – for relevant investment. One of the best TED talks on narrative by numbers (Hans Rosling aside) was given in April 2015 by self-confessed "data storyteller" Ben Wellington.[3] Wellington fell into his role almost accidentally, spurred into action by Mayor Bloomberg's decision to create an open data portal[4] that made all of the city's data sets publicly available. At the time the TED talk was recorded, the data portal already had 1,200 data sets, but the repository is now several times larger.

- **Weather and holiday data** – Many organisations – particularly retailers and branded goods companies – rely on weather data to plan and predict demand. From DIY outlets to ice cream manufacturers, weather data can be incredibly helpful in building data-driven stories.
- **Academic data** – All U.K. academic institutions and many research labs make much of their data available for public access, partly for scrutiny and partly to stimulate collaboration.
- **Drug trial data** – After controversies about pharma companies and university research labs only publishing the results of trials that report favourable outcomes for their drugs, there has been a move on both sides of the research divide to make trial data publicly available.
- **Other data** – The U.K. Office of National Statistics is a great repository of data that details trends and developments in what the U.K. population is like. Crime, vehicle ownership, pet ownership, religion, sexuality. Whatever you want to know about the people of Great Britain, it's probably there. Including the fact that Brighton is the hotbed of the Jedi "religion", at least according to the most recent U.K. census, taken in 2011.

So, not only are there vast quantities of data available inside most organisations, there is also a mass of publicly available data. Taken together, these data sets can make it difficult to know where to start and which data sets to use as the foundation of your narrative. Because of the seemingly endless availability of different types of data, it's also incredibly easy – and even more tempting – to throw everything into the mix and go on what statisticians calling a fishing expedition.

Fishing expeditions are dangerous, because if you start with no idea of what you want to get out of your data analysis and you're just letting the data do the storytelling, two things are likely to happen. First, you'll get an answer of some sort. And second, the answer is likely to be attractive – "Why didn't I think of that? How couldn't I see that?" But third, it's also most likely to be wrong.

When looking for relationships between data sets – between specific variables, say social media sentiment and sales – the standard tools available to the inquisitive, stats-literate storyteller are correlation and, building on that technique, regression analysis. Don't get me wrong. This isn't a stats textbook. There are many excellent stats textbooks available, including almost anything written by one of my former stats teachers at the University of Sussex, Andy Field.[5] But bear with me on this line of thought for just three short paragraphs more. Or skip past them if they make you break out in a cold sweat.

Correlation looks at sets of numbers and asks these sets of numbers if there's a relationship of any sort between them. In the case of social media sentiment and sales, for instance, do sales go up when people say more nice things about us, do sales go down when people say more nasty things about us, or is there no direct, obvious relationship. Relationships can be linear (direct) and positive (one goes up while the other goes up) or negative (one goes up while the other goes down). Relationships can also be cubic or quadratic – there are twists in the tale. In our example, it might be that sales go up when people say nice things about us, but when the sentiment gets too sickly sweet, people cease believing that the comments are authentic and suspect them to be astroturfing (fake posts engineered behind the scenes by the company), and sales go down (a cubic relationship).

Life isn't usually that simple, however. One thing doesn't usually cause another in the absence of any other factors. As we considered in the introduction, as cognitive creatures, we are attracted to single-factor solutions. We find multiple factors, interacting with each other, difficult to grasp. Or at least we find it difficult to hold all these factors in mind simultaneously: "This if that and that but not the other". So, while some might want to put Leicester City's 2015/16 Premiership success down to Claudio Ranieri's management – and the club's owners certainly thought he was the single cause of failure, when they sacked him just eight months later – there were likely many other, interacting factors behind that extraordinary 5,000–1 success.

So, because life is more complicated than single-factor solutions, statisticians have developed more complex statistical tests that we can use to look at relationships between multiple different factors. We can see what the relationship is like between multiple predictor variables (variables that predict an outcome) and an outcome variable (the impact of the inputs). There are different techniques – including regression analysis and analysis of variance (ANOVA), cluster analysis, and factor analysis – but they all, at their heart, use correlations between variables to work out their answers.

(FAO statistophobes – it's safe to come back now). For the organisational storyteller, correlating different variables together can be a dangerous thing. Going back to our example of social media and sales, this is likely to be too simple a model, as we'll explore shortly. But before we get there, it may well be that such a simple model fails to consider the impact of a hidden third cause.

Imagine you're the brand manager of a new ice cream sandwich brand. You notice an increase in the number of social media mentions – and in the number of positive mentions – for your product. This follows investment in a dynamic campaign with a hot new social media agency, and it's really bearing fruit. Over the same period, you track an increase in your sales and also in the number of new vendors looking to stock your product.

You conclude that positive social media comment has driven sales and distribution, report this to the marketing director, and ask for more budget for the social media agency. And then feel incredibly deflated when she points out that the period in question was spring into summer, and you've failed to account for the hidden third cause: the weather. Her greater experience immediately tells her that people tweet more about ice cream brands – more positively – because they are more present in the lives of consumers when it gets hotter. Rather than causing the increase in sales, the increase in positive social media mentions were most likely the result of more people buying and eating the product because May, June, and July are warmer than February, March, and April.

Before you dismiss this analysis as fanciful and naive, a word of warning. I've seen exactly these kinds of conclusions drawn time and again because organisations tried to draw too-simple, one-factor models of the world and ignored perhaps the most obvious cause, a hidden third factor, which has an obvious impact on both the other variables in the correlation. It was tempting for our brand manager to look at social media sentiment and sales, because he wanted to justify his investment decision and get more budget for his favoured agency. He would have been better off looking at a thermometer and a calendar. How analogue!

Fishing expeditions can also be dangerous because they represent an incomplete model of the world that doesn't take in all the relevant variables. Even if you build a regression analysis with what you believe – and history has shown – to be the five most important predictors of sales, you may well be leaving out the most important factor. Like the advertising spend of an aggressive new competitor in the market which, while you don't control it, turns out to be the decisive factor in your shrinking market share. Not your middle managers' average waistline, the price of stamps, or the impact of new Government legislation.

Finally, fishing expeditions are a classic example of what I first heard Andy Field describe as GIGO: Garbage In, Garbage Out. There is so much data available to all sorts of organisations today – companies, brands, charities, NGOs, Government departments, academics, journalists, bloggers, politicians, religious leaders . . . frankly, to everyone. The tools to undertake even rudimentary data analysis are also ubiquitous. I'm not talking expensive applications like Tableau, great as they are. I'm talking applications on every Mac and PC I've ever seen, Numbers and Excel. So, the data and the tools are at everyone's disposal. But there isn't necessarily the critical faculty or the training to judge whether the correlation you're running is likely to produce meaningful – let alone true – results.

SPURIOUS CORRELATIONS

Tyler Vigen is a student at Harvard Law School. He became so obsessed with the spurious correlations he saw appearing across news and social media – and a little distracted from his law studies – that he started downloading a wealth of different, publicly available data sets. He then ran endless correlations to make the point – in a very funny, quasi-academic way – that just because you can correlate two sets of data with one another it doesn't mean that you should. More importantly, it doesn't necessarily reveal anything meaningful. He's brought together hundreds of data sets and produced literally tens of thousands of charts that show very strong relationships – technically very strong correlation coefficients or r values – between the most unlikely of variables.

Some of the most memorable are collected in a book, *Spurious Correlations*, that you should buy. My favourites include:

- U.S. spending on science, space, and technology and suicides by hanging, strangling, and suffocation (r = 0.99)
- Age of Miss America and murders by steam, hot vapours, and hot objects (r = 0.87)
- Math doctorates awarded and uranium stored at U.S. nuclear power stations (r = 0.95)

And this one, below: the number of people who drowned by falling into a pool and films Nicolas Cage appeared in (r = 0.67). A comparatively weak correlation, but WHAT a story! Oh . . .

On his open-access website – and I challenge you not to get lost for hours at tylervigen.com/spurious-correlations – Vigen says of himself:

> I love to wonder about how variables work together. The charts on this site aren't meant to imply causation nor are they meant to create a distrust for research or even correlative data. Rather, I hope this project fosters interest in statistics and numerical research.

What the book says loud and clear – and it's a statistical lesson even the least numerate appear to have heard – is that . . .

Correlation is not the same as causation

. . . a lesson that even the more numerate are sometimes too quick to forget when they've been on a fishing expedition and found something apparently interesting.

The satirical online publication *The Onion* regularly plays with data-driven storytelling, has a fondness for the spurious correlation, and a

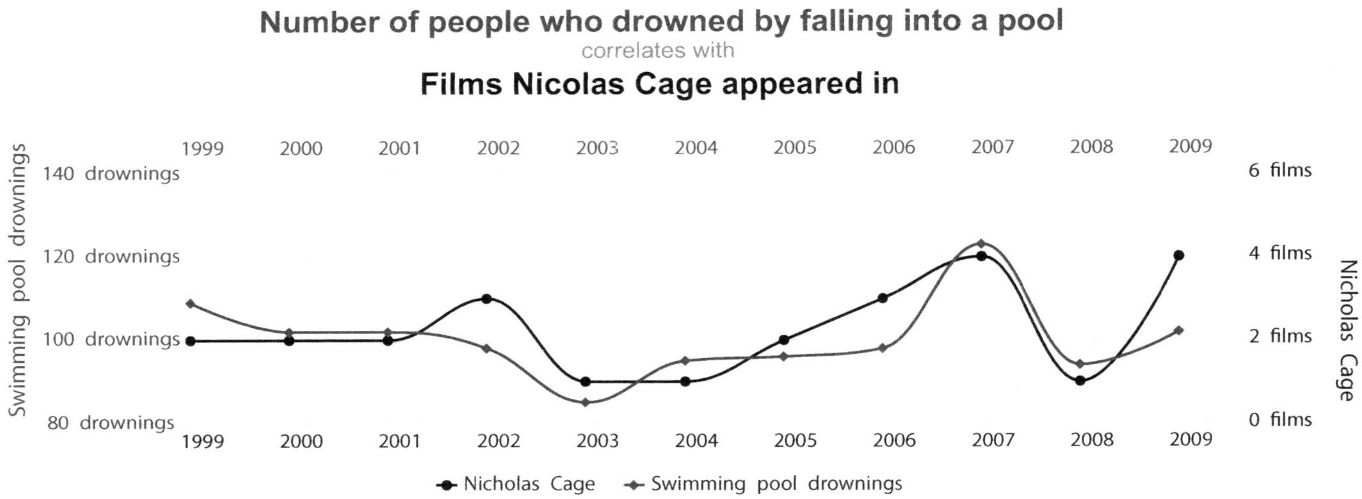
Number of people who drowned by falling into a pool
correlates with
Films Nicolas Cage appeared in
1999
2000
2001
2002
2003
2004
2005
2006
2007
2008
2009
Swimming pool drownings
140 drownings
120 drownings
100 drownings
80 drownings
6 films
4 films
2 films
0 films
Nicholas Cage
Nicholas Cage
Swimming pool drownings

Figure 3.1 Spurious correlation (second chart)

particular penchant for drawing precisely the opposite conclusion from the "research findings" they present to build bogus news stories. One recent gem reported:[6] "Study finds exposure to violent children causes increased aggression in video game characters". Quite so.

In the end, it all comes down to what you want to find out, what story you're looking to tell, and which data and statistics you can best use to help tell that story. When looking to select the right data to be the underpinning of your story, you need to start with a meaningful hypothesis you wish to test with the data. And not – as is too often the case, particularly on fishing expeditions – start with the data and see what it says. Worse yet, start with a conclusion in mind and see if you can't bend the data to support the case you're trying to make.

This is not the approach that (proper) scientists take with data when they use data to test hypotheses. Tempting as it may be – particularly if it's building on a body of existing work – scientists don't look to prove their hypotheses, they look to test them. They look to see if, by experimental manipulation – say giving drug x – they can rule out everything apart from the dosage of the drug as being the cause of the outcome they record – say better memory for faces. The intelligent use of statistics to rule everything out – and conclude that it's likely to be the impact of your experimental manipulation that's had the effect – is known as null-hypothesis significance testing. The null hypothesis is the devil's advocate position, assuming what you were testing didn't happen. Organisational storytellers would be well advised to take this approach, too, when looking to build an evidence-based story. Or otherwise you'll make the philosopher Karl Popper, the father of the scientific method, spin in his grave.

DETECTING THE SIGNAL FROM THE NOISE

Nate Silver is one of the gods of predictive analytics. He and his 538 team have a near-legendary reputation for predicting the outcomes of elections and sporting fixtures. Together, they make deep and deeply intelligent use of data and statistics to show what's likely to happen next. Their skills netted Silver star contracts with first the *New York Times* as the home for the 538 blog, focused on political forecasting, and then at ESPN.

In the 2008 and 2012 U.S. presidential elections, Silver correctly predicted the right result in almost every congressional district for the two Obama presidential victories. And while the polling and predictive analytics business was thrown two curve balls by both the EU Referendum and the 2016 U.S. presidential race, it's fair to say that on both those elections Silver and his team were among the least wrong.

Silver leapt from specialist to generalist interest with the publication of his 2013 book, *The Signal and the Noise*. The title neatly captures what organisational leaders are looking to distil and to discard when choosing the right data and using the right statistics to analyse that data to tell better, data-driven stories. All the different categories of organisational and publicly available data listed above (pp. 49–52) offer the opportunity, if treated right, to detect meaningful signals. Signals that form the foundations and the underpinning of more impactful, evidence-based storytelling. But approached with insufficient caution, they are more likely to generate meaningless noise.

Many organisational leaders have been poorly served during the Big Data revolution. Data has been disunited, when an integrated view would tell a more complete story. Casual observations are slapped onto apparent trends too early and with insufficient caution. Hypotheses aren't tested; the data is manipulated to prove a point. Small "p" politics wins out over statistical rigour. And the lure of the all-singing, all-dancing data visualisation dashboard has spawned an industry but afflicted organisations with too many pretty ways of making no sense of nothing.

Taken together, disunited data sets, casual observations, hypothesis hijacking, and Dashboard Syndrome are unhelpful at best, counter-productive at worst. The prescription of better data-driven storytelling starts with knowing where to look, what to look for, and who to have on the team.

Pierre Emmanuel Maire is the advertising planner responsible for the compelling "Dirt Is Good" insight that helped Unilever take global leadership from Procter & Gamble in the laundry category. Ever since the invention and mass production of washing powder – including the development of the soap opera as an advertising vehicle for P&G's products in the 1920s – advertisers had done little more than make mums feel guilty. The "whiter than white" advertising shtick had been the category norm for decades, implying only just beneath the surface that a mum was a bad mum if her kids' clothes weren't always spotless. As if dads had any role in doing the washing . . .

"Dirt Is Good" turns this idea on its head – as well as empowering parents to allow their kids to express themselves, enabling kids to be kids and get outside and play. Yes, Unilever's laundry products like Persil and Skip will get the kids' clothes clean – of course it will, that's why the product exists. But rather than constrain children's growing and learning opportunities found rolling and romping around in the mud, eating a peck of dirt, "Dirt Is Good" as a message enables parents (not just mums!) to forget about the clothes-cleaning part, because that's already taken care of.

Maire distilled the insight from research he led at ad agency Ammirati Puris Lintas. In an interview with me conducted in September 2015, he described finding the right nuggets of data like prospecting for oil. "Unearthing genuine insights is like finding oil. First, you *zone* in the right area. Next, you *mine* in the right place. Then, you *extract* something relatively crude. And finally, you *refine* it until you have something powerful."

SUMMING UP

The Bigness of Big Data can be intimidating.

Use your resources to identify the corner of little big data that holds the answers to the questions you want to ask.

Tools and techniques – from Boolean logic to big data analytics – are important. But it's not, first and foremost, a technology problem. It's a more problem of purpose – of identifying and articulating your purpose or your "Why?", as Simon Sinek shows so elegantly in his 2009 TED Talk.

To ask the right questions that will deliver the right data and statistics, you need to work bottom up, not top down.

This is true for social media analytics, for market research, for any means you may choose to identify and isolate the right data and statistics.

Done right, social media analytics can represent the most natural and unfiltered form of market research available.

There's a huge amount of data available to all organisations – data inside the organisation, and also massive, publicly available data sets. You should embrace the wealth of available data, but always be on the lookout for the false positive.

Statistical fishing expeditions involve setting off into the great unknown of available data and seeing what you can find. Not to be recommended.

Outcomes very rarely have single causes, particularly in complex markets or environments. The problem with building statistical models of the world – particularly when looking for cause and effect – is that you leave out or ignore relevant data sources.

Correlation very definitely does not equal causation. While spurious correlations are often hilarious, they're very rarely helpful. Except when you want to talk about how unhelpful they are.

When looking to test (not prove) hypotheses, use the scientific method and deploy null-hypothesis significance testing. With this approach, you're looking to rule out every possible cause of the outcome you've observed before accepting it was something you did to try to change things.

Detecting the signal from the noise is a holy grail, but many leaders have been let down by disunited data sets, casual observations, and the debilitating affliction known as Dashboard Syndrome.

To get a head start in data-driven storytelling, take leaf out of the oil discovery business. Zone in the right area, mine in the right place, extract something relatively crude, and then refine it until you have something powerful.

GIVE IT A GO: WHAT MAKES THE NEWS?

Take two newspapers, one more upmarket (in the U.K., perhaps the *Daily Telegraph;* in the U.S., maybe the *New York Times*), one more downmarket (in the U.K., perhaps the *Daily Mail;* in the U.S., maybe *USA Today*). You could use the online versions – which carry more stories – but there's something incredibly satisfying about doing this exercise with a newspaper (while they still last) and scissors.

Scan every story for data-driven stories. The City and financial pages are always full of annual or quarterly results, news of mergers and acquisitions, and financial performance metrics. That's a relatively easy place to start. But keep on reading, starting wherever you want, and you'll be amazed to find quite how important data and statistics are to news. Government figures, the results of new research, the impact of Big Data, the potential of Blockchain or its new challenger Hashgraph, the number of passes completed by the star of your favourite football team . . . anything you choose to mention.

Cut out all articles that are data-driven, and make a tally of the proportion of stories that depend on data to make their points. Advanced players of this game should focus on a data-driven story in an area with which they're incredibly familiar, and here a web search will likely prove more fruitful. Find a story about your organisation or its category but not generated by it; choose one generated by or about a competitor or peer. And then really work at the data and statistics, and assess how true or accurate you believe the story to be.

DATA-DRIVEN STORIES

Producers As Heroes

What's the organisation?
Tesco, the U.K.'s largest supermarket. In October 2016, it had 28% market share, accounting for around one in eight of every pound spent on the high street.

What's the brand?
Corporate brand – Tesco food, across all categories

What's the campaign?
Producers As Heroes

What's the story?
To change perceptions about the quality of Tesco's produce, the company made a strategic shift to champion the stories of the producers – from farmers to bakers, from whisky distillers to vegetable growers.

How did data drive the story?
The campaign was born from a linguistic frequency analysis of a Tesco customer competition and the tie-breaker line "[PRODUCT X] is my favourite, quality Tesco product because . . .". Contestants had 30 words or fewer to say why.

What was the outcome of the campaign?
Fundamental and sustained shift in perceptions of Tesco as a provider of quality products.

On returning from summer holidays in 2010, the most intriguing email trail I found in my inbox connected me to Tesco's then ad agency, Red Brick Road. Now this is long before retailing's tallest poppy hit the buffers, chewed through CEOs, made some of the biggest losses in British corporate history, and got mired in accounting scandals. The recession had started to change the dynamics of food shopping – Aldi and Lidl were making waves, Waitrose had launched an Essentials range, and everyone was parking tanks on their competitors' lawns.

Tesco, I learned from the emails, was starting to talk about quality. They'd developed some farm gate to store stories and begun advertising about the quality of food not just in its Finest* range. But it wasn't cutting through in earned media; in news, broadcast, and social. Expecting journalists, bloggers, and punters to suddenly start talking and writing about the quality of Tesco's products just wasn't a realistic aspiration, at least not with the strategy they were pursuing.

With colleagues, I took what proved to be the first of many trains for the next two years to Cheshunt, met the food marketing supremos and category heads, and headed back to the office with a bag full of briefing materials. Least promising of all was a fat spreadsheet full of competition entries from Tesco customers (always customers; never consumers or clients). The competition theme? "What's your favourite quality Tesco product?" Tiebreaker? "[PRODUCT X] is my favourite, quality Tesco product because . . .". Tens of thousands had taken the time to enter, but the marketers didn't know what to do with all their comments and nominations.

That night – and it did take all night – I subjected the spreadsheet to intensive linguistic analysis, crunching frequencies of words and looking at how customers talked about their favourite quality Tesco products. And the new day began, I had a sense that this unpromising spreadsheet might hold the key to unlocking the brief of getting journalists and social media commentators – yes, even in 2010 – to talk about the quality of Tesco's food, challenging misconceptions and building an already shaky reputation. The linguistic analysis revealed four important traits underpinning customers' opinions about what set their favourite Tesco's food apart: Britishness, freshness, produced on farms, and taste. But the traits felt more like indicators than insight; like filtered data than a central idea on which to base a campaign about quality.

Stuck, I took a timeout. Timeout is one of the most important and underestimated tools in idea creation and insight generation. Deliberately taking time away from the problem you're trying to solve allows the subconscious mind to do that brilliant thing it does all the time without you even noticing: recombination. Vilfredo Pareto may be best known for his 80/20 rule. But his second most famous maxim is: "An idea is nothing more or less than a combination of old elements". How right he is.

The subconscious glues together already-acquired information (read here data and statistics) and puts them together in new and interesting ways. Many, it will reject. But some it will promote and when they pop through into consciousness that, for me, is the very essence of the eureka moment. (I'll talk much more about this in my next book, *How to Be Insightful*).

So, stuck, I went to meet a collaborator at the Rude Britannia exhibition at Tate Britain. This celebration of Anglo-Saxon smut, from saucy seaside postcards to the *Carry On* franchise, was a romp through what tickled Britain's rude funny bone from the World War II onwards. And it was while taking this timeout, wandering between the giant blow-ups of pages of *Viz Comic*, that I realised I'd worked it out. I had my eureka moment. Three metres tall, giant blow-ups of two *Viz* characters – Farmer Palmer (catchphrase "Get off moi land!") and 8 Ace (alcoholic superhero) – towered over me. And suddenly, the idle chit-chat with my collaborator stopped. Combining the traits from the linguistic analysis with these two characters, I had my insight.

To tell the Tesco quality story – about tasty, fresh, British food that Tesco customers loved so much – we needed to tell the story through the eyes of the farmers who supplied produce for the supermarket. Not Farmer Palmer, but Tesco farmers. Yes, the products were sold at Tesco, but the true heroes were the farmers and growers and producers who made such good quality produce. Tesco was the enabler, the facilitator, and not just to quality food products on the shelves today, but also to growing thousands of other businesses across the country whose quality food products they distribute and sell.

And so was born Producers As Heroes, an award-winning campaign that lasted 18 months and helped to reposition Tesco and challenge three misperceptions it had struggled to throw off.

1   That Tesco's products – outside its Finest* range – were generally pretty poor quality.
2   That Tesco's relationship with its producers was one-way traffic and in no way a partnership. The shorthand outside the business was that Tesco used to "screw its suppliers to the floor".
3   That Tesco's unique size and reach were a force for good for Tesco and Tesco only.

The campaign was not, of course, robust enough to withstand the challenges that came to disrupt Tesco so profoundly after Terry Leahy left and Philip Clarke took over, before Dave Lewis steadied the ship as CEO. A communications campaign could never withstand the collapse of Tesco's U.S. expansion plans via Fresh 'n' Easy, the onslaught of the discounters, and internal accounting scandals. But for a good 18 months – while the data-driven storymining and storytelling team went through all of Tesco's different categories and found and told great data-driven stories – the food marketing business helped to change what many people said and then thought about Tesco.

> *Key takeaway*: Sometimes, the data and statistics you need to tell powerful stories are sitting right underneath your nose. Turning data into insights and insights into compelling stories requires both analytical skills and storytelling nous.

NOTES

1   A good example of their generosity in content marketing – and an excellent resource for analysing Twitter content – is their 2016 blog *The Top 10 Free Twitter Analytics Tools*, linked here http://bit.ly/2q23EPf
2   See www.gapminder.org, so-named because of the paternalistic warning on the London Underground. More about Hans Rosling and his work in Chapter 7.

3 "Making data mean more through storytelling" by Ben Wellington (2015, April 20) TEDxBroadway. http://bit.ly/1XzrMAd

4 https://opendata.cityofnewyork.us

5 www.discoveringstatistics.com

6 www.theonion.com/article/study-finds-exposure-violent-children-causes-in-cre-55456

4

THE FOUR Es OF EFFECTIVE STORYTELLING

Stories are powerful ways of connecting emotionally with your audience.
Dale Carnegie (1915), *The Art of Public Speaking*

DRIVING ENGAGEMENT

The holy grail of marketing – particularly digital marketing, and most particularly social media marketing – is engagement. The two-way, conversational nature of social media enables companies and brands to see in real time how people are responding to what they're saying and doing. Not only does social media provide an immediate feedback loop, it also comes with built-in measurement and metrics that can – used right – help organisations understand in more detail the extent to which they have genuinely engaged current and potential customers.

If individuals share content produced by companies or brands on their personal timelines or feeds without comment, the creator of that content can assume that the person doing the sharing believes it's worth sharing. They can't be certain that they like or approve of the content – they might be sharing it without comment to a loyal following who all know, without accompanying editorial commentary, that a share means "look at what these idiots are saying now". This trope is common when sharing content from contentious politicians and journalists (think Donald Trump and Katie Hopkins, though both of them often have abuse added at the top of a share or retweet).

But in general, when an individual shares content put out by an organisation, it's fairly safe to assume that the person sharing approves of the content they're passing on. The act of sharing anything involves attaching a little piece of the person sharing to the content shared. In the least active way possible, they're endorsing what they're sharing by saying to their followers, "I think you should look at this, too".

If the person doing the sharing actively likes or favourites content from an organisation, the organisation can assume with greater confidence that they approve of the content. And if people share content and add a comment, the words, phrases, and sentiment used alongside the share give companies and brands a good idea of what they actually thought about the content they're sharing. Of course, people often share or retweet and add a hostile comment (think Trump and Hopkins again), but the fresh content on top of the original content makes it completely transparent what the sharer intends by sharing.

The act of sharing is actually comparatively rare. It is estimated that even the most active Twitter users, for instance, only see a maximum of 4% of all tweets that pass over their timeline from those accounts they follow. It is rare for users to like or retweet more than 1% of those tweets they do see, except in the special case of fans of celebrities, who often like and retweet almost everything a Justin Bieber or a Katie Perry ever posts.

When a Twitter user does retweet or like tweets, these have the potential to be seen by that user's followers, though based on the 4% figure above, if a given user has 1,000 followers, no more than 40 of them would be expected to see the like or retweet. Social media engagement can quickly become a game of diminishing returns.

Because social and digital media channels are still relatively young, and because companies, brands, and other organisations using them are mostly fairly naive about what engagement is and what drives it, a good number of third-party businesses have been set up to measure and report on engagement. The products and services these companies offer can map how far particular pieces of content travel, the extent to which they're shared, how many people they have reached, and so how engaging the content is deemed to be. Just take what they say with a pinch of salt, particularly the unjustifiably ubiquitous Klout score.

There are three challenges with the engagement scores and ratings these companies provide:

1   They are usually only absolute and not relative, and there's no sense about what is a good engagement score and what is not so good.
2   These measurement systems are measures of potential communications output, not outcomes. They don't report on what's been achieved by the tweet or blog post, just how far it's travelled and, potentially, how many people could have seen it.
3   Many of the most-used social media platforms – including Facebook, Instagram, Snapchat, and Google+ – operate as "walled gardens", and no-one has access to even output data apart from the platforms owners themselves.

Several times in 2016 and 2017, Facebook has been forced to admit that it has overestimated how many people were exposed to ads and videos on its platform, and for how long. It has also been compelled to revise down potential audience reach because it has declared figures for – say – teens in the U.K. and U.S. that are higher than the total populations provided in census data.

THE POWER OF ENGLISH

When looking to prepare powerful, data-driven stories that are likely to drive engagement in a target audience, it is important to ensure that the content organisations prepare and distribute is fit for purpose. English is such a rich language with gloriously diverse ways of saying the same thing. In one form or another, English has been around for more than a millennium. In that time, many other languages – of conquerors and the conquered, of allies and foes – have left their trace. That's why we have rusks and biscuits, crackers and cookies cheek-by-jowl in the same supermarket aisle.

You see, English – unlike rather too many of its native speakers on its home island these days – is an incredibly welcoming entity, willing to admit as many chambers as it does verandas, as happy with Schadenfreude as the Kindergarten. Mercifully there is no Academie Anglaise, and our linguistic open borders policy allows us to build narratives – tell tales – fabricate fables from the richest palate available to storytellers anywhere.

One benefit of this tolerance for tautology is that the able English speaker can deploy more forms of speech than those less linguistically well-endowed. And one of the simplest and most pleasing to the ear is alliteration: starting successive words with the same letter or sound, creating a rhythmic cadence to phrasing to make it more memorable. It's not a bad starting point.

What's more, research from the pre-digital age – particularly from the laboratories of Paul Ekman at the University of California at San Francisco, where he created a universal *Atlas of Emotions* – mean that we know that people pay more attention to information that ticks the following three boxes.

1   It's *emotional* – it covers emotional subject areas and it triggers the emotions.
2   Connected to this, it needs to be *energetic*. Language – and, luckily for me and us, particularly the English language – is able to convey energy and excite, even on the printed page, even on the shimmering screen of a computer, a tablet, or a phone.
3   It's *empathetic* – it considers the world from the point of view of those it's trying to influence. It talks to the target audience in the language they understand and respond to.

EMOTION

Data-driven stories that include an emotional element are actually remembered better than those stories that are purely factual. This is true of both positive and negative stories, both of which are more memorable than neutral, fact-based stories. This is because words and concepts that trigger an emotional response are of evolutionary value. Those things you could eat, mate with, or be killed by, deserve and command our attention, and should not be forgotten. What's been dubbed the brain's emotional barometer, an oval body called the amygdala (amygdala is the Greek for "almond") lights up when we see, hear, talk about, or observe something pleasant or unpleasant.

The amygdala (actually, there are two of them; just drill in on either side from the eyes and ears and the amygdalae are at the meeting point) is an ancient structure. It's the keystone of the limbic system – also known as the emotional brain – and is something we share with many other animal groups, including reptiles, birds, and, of course, other mammals. Emotional content is encoded more deeply, more richly through the involvement of the amygdala, and as a result is remembered better. Organisations would do well to remember this lesson from Psychology 101.

During the EU Referendum campaign, Vote Leave campaigner Michael Gove claimed, "people in this country have had enough of experts". His contention was in response to the Remain campaign's constant use of dry facts and data about what might or might not happen to the economy in the event that Britain left the EU.

In the aftermath of Vote Leave's success, there has been a lot of debate about whether we have entered a "post-truth society". The *Guardian*[1] reported on 19 September 2016: "The rush to believe that facts and evidence aren't what people want is already streaming through policy and professional circles and influencing a rethink of how to communicate with the public." This debate was redoubled after the 2016 U.S. presidential election, during which truth and facts apparently played a less important role than fake news. "Post-truth" was even the Oxford English Dictionary's "word" of the year in 2016.[2]

The evidence suggests that it is not that facts are irrelevant, that we have not, indeed, entered a "post-truth society". In fact, we live in an age when facts have never mattered more, as we'll explore in Chapter 8. But what is also undeniable is that facts – data and statistics – need to be delivered with emotional relevance and resonance. Simply trying to change someone's mind by (a) telling them they're wrong and (b) showing them the facts that prove they're wrong is counter-productive. In fact, using such a laboured, expository storytelling style is more likely to make them become further entrenched in contrary views. And as well as an emotional veneer, data-driven corporate and brand storytellers need a dose of intrigue to stimulate further interest.

The "post-truth society" is a particular nightmare vision for the scientific community, whose whole raison d'être is to underpinned by knowledge, facts, data, and statistics. In a rallying cry editorial written just after the referendum, *New Scientist* magazine wrote:[3] "For reason to triumph, scientists need to learn to engage with emotion."

ENERGY

English is a vibrant, living, ever-changing beast. All languages are, but English is particularly adaptable, capable of expressing energy through the types of words and phrases you choose to tell your data-driven story. It's also supremely flexible. Has rules just waiting to broken. Smashed; crashed. Dashed against the rocks. Completeness comes from full sentences. But also from shards. Jagged outcrops.

What's more, different types of words convey different states: verbs for action (think sports reporting), nouns for facts (an engineering manual), and adjectives for emotion (rousing poetry). And we've already set out above why emotion is so important in data-driven storytelling.

Too factual (the usual failing)? Cut down the noun count, particularly Latinate, abstract nouns.

Not enough action? More punchy, Germanic verbs please. Contrast the deathly dull "preparation, incubation, illumination, and verification" with the raw energy of "sweat, timeout, eureka, prove". And how would you like a perfect first date to end? Would you rather osculate, kiss, or even snog? Same ideas, very different levels of engagement through emotion.

Content lacking in emotional appeal? Increase the number and intensity of adjectives. Two is too few, four is a list, but three has the potential to become a mind worm. Three adjectives like emotional, energetic, and empathetic, say.

EMPATHY

The Cocktail Party Rule states: "If you want to be boring, talk about your-self. But if you want to be interesting, talk about what matters to those who are listening." Just consider those who draw an audience at a party, like bees round a honeypot. Are they talking about themselves? Almost never. They're talking about a subject and in a manner that draws others in.

To achieve this with impact means thinking from others' points of view before we start talking – before we start telling our data-driven stories. It means understanding how others will receive the information that's transmitted, not just thinking about the elegance of transmission. And being able to do this is only possible to the mind readers among us – the truly empathetic. Well come back to the Cocktail Party Rule in Chapter 6.

We met the New York–based data storyteller, Ben Wellington, in Chap-ter 2. In addition to the helpful provision of public data sets by Mayor Bloomberg's open data laws providing raw, Big Data sets for Wellington to work with, his skills as a data storyteller have benefitted hugely from his track record in improvisational theatre and comedy, or improv. As he explains in his TEDxBroadway talk, improv is all about telling stories better and connecting with people's experiences through empathy.

The skilled improv performer doesn't look to tell his or her own story; he or she looks to riff off what co-performers are doing and saying, and the best way to anticipate even a nonsense scene is to use empathy to understand the other characters. As Dan Pink shows in *To Sell Is Human*, great improv performers see every scene as an opportunity for empa-thetic, two-way dialogue. They see every line from another performer as an invitation. And this makes them approach their responses with an open attitude of "Yes, and . . ." rather than the closed and restricting "No, but . . ." Additionally, improv requires performers to focus on single ideas, keep scenes simple, and explore subject areas that performers know best. But above anything else, successful improv comes from empathy, which is also a core skill of the organisational storyteller.

In the case of organisations telling data-driven stories, looking to engage in dialogue with customers and consumers, empathy is a skill to be sought out, learned, and prized. Those organisations that fail to put themselves in the shoes of their audience, who can't see – and tell – stories from their perspective, well, they're suffering from what we might call corporate Asperger's syndrome. Some are mildly on the spectrum and just a little mind-blind. They can learn shortcuts to overcome this condition. But others – often business-to-business, tech-first enterprises – can only see the world from their perspective and need fundamental rewiring if they're ever to be thought of as engaging.

ENGAGEMENT

The fundamental point of any storytelling, of any language you choose to use, is to interest and attract those you want to influence. In the always-on world of corporate and brand dialogue, this applies as much to companies as it always has to people. And organisations can learn to talk that elusive dialect of English – Human – if they follow the golden rules of storytelling.

If they wear their hearts on their sleeve and display their **emotion**.

If they keep up the pace and exhibit real **energy**.

If they put themselves in their audience's shoes and reveal their **empathy**.

Do all of these things, and you're very much more likely to secure that elusive fourth E: **engagement**.

SUMMING UP

The power of story has been known from the time of Aristotle onwards, and was first recommended to business leaders for more than a century in Dale Carnegie's seminal *The Art of Public Speaking*.

Every organisation craves engagement from those it seeks to influence.

When people share content from an organisation, it's a pretty good sign they want to draw others' attention to that content.

When they comment favourably on content they share, it's safe to assume they approve of what they're sharing and the organisation. They're already one of your advocates.

Sharing and liking are remarkably rare.

People pay more attention to content if it's emotional (not – just – rational), if it's energetic (not passive), and if it's empathetic (not self-absorbed).

Emotional stories are more richly and deeply encoded in memory than facts alone. They trigger the brain's emotional barometer, the amygdala.

Facts matter, but facts need to be placed in the context of human emotions.

English is particularly versatile in the way it can convey energy to meaning. Nouns deliver facts, verbs action, and adjectives emotion.

Organisations need to tell stories with the audience in mind. They need their empathy radar switched on and working.

Engagement is a consequence of emotion, energy, and empathy.

GIVE IT A GO: NOUNS, VERBS, AND ADJECTIVES

Go back to your organisation's About Us page. Or, if you don't work for an organisation, go to the About Us page of an organisation you admire. Capture the text into a Pages or Word file. Strip out all of the words apart from nouns, verbs, and adjectives. Then tally these up. Which comes out on top?

Mostly nouns, and the organisation values facts and information most highly.

Mostly verbs, and the organisation is a go-getter. (Though if they're mostly in the passive voice "the shop was opened" rather than "we opened the shop" it's not that go-getting).

And mostly adjectives, this is an organisation that wears its heart on its sleeve. It understands how to communicate emotion.

Does the relative count of nouns, verbs, and adjectives for the organisation in question meet your expectations of what it's actually like? If not – and particularly if it's your organisation – rewrite the About Us page to match either the reality or the desired perception, and share it with those who can bring about change.

Alternatively, get a group of people from your organisation together. Working in teams of four or five, generate three lists of 20–30 nouns, adjectives, and verbs that are truly distinctive to your organisation – why it exists, what it does, and how it does it.

Then, take it in turns to make sentences that describe the organisation using at least one of each. It'll be like wading through treacle and feel unnatural at first. But after a few minutes of playing with your distinctive lexicon, it'll feel good and empowering. And you'll be surprised at how good it sounds – and consistently so.

DATA-DRIVEN STORIES

Dear Person

What's the organisation?
Spotify
What's the brand?
Music streaming service
What's the campaign?
Dear Person
What's the story?
Develop locally tailored advertising in markets around the world based on the music Spotify knows its users have been streaming in particular countries, cities, or markets.
How did data drive the story?
The campaign could not have existed without the data, statistics, and analytics.
What was the outcome of the campaign?
Increase in empathy and understanding between users and Spotify. And a milestone achievement of passing 40m subscribers at the end of 2016.

Spotify is the Stockholm-headquartered music streaming system that has revolutionised people's relationship with music around the world. Although music streaming systems existed before Spotify (most notably Napster) and although big players who are never first to market but often swoop in and clean up have since launched their own music streaming services (most notably Apple with its Apple Music platform), Spotify is the dominant player in the market, across multiple markets.

There are a number of reasons why Spotify has proven to be so successful. The company has been able to sign up the vast majority of record labels and artists whose music is in demand. They have made it simple and straightforward to no longer own physical copies of music but rather to pay to have access to digital copies, streaming seamlessly between devices. They provide different levels of membership, from free (with ads every 30 minutes), small monthly payment (on a handful of devices and streaming on only one at a time), and slightly larger monthly payment (multiple – family – users, streaming simultaneously). At every step of the way, Spotify has used its technology and data management to drive success.

In order to pay micro-royalties every time an artist's music is streamed, Spotify knows who has streamed the music, where (geographically), on what type of device, at what time, and whether they've done so just once or repeatedly. Not only does this enable them to know how much they need to pay to licence and copyright holders of music, but it also enables them to make suggestions and recommendations, from new artists to user-created playlists, as well as offering special offers for concert tickets and meet-and-greets to committed fans who stream particular artists the most.

As a truly data-driven business, Spotify chose to use what it knows about its users' streaming behaviour as the fuel for a global advertising campaign towards the end of 2016. Without seeing the creative executions, in principle this campaign sounds dull and dry – just a data-driven communications campaign that reflects back to users what they've been doing.

In reality, the delivery of Spotify's "Dear Person" campaign follows the principles of the 4Es of storytelling. To drive user engagement – and also, without doubt, to trigger subscribers to reach for phones and tablets and stream some more – the witty executions play on emotion, use real energy, and display deep empathy.

Campaign posters, which ran from November 2016, first in the U.K., France, Germany, and the U.S., and then in ten more countries, included the headlines:

> *"Dear person who played Sorry 42 times on Valentine's Day. What did you do?"*
>
> *"Dear 3,749 people who streamed* It's The End of the World As We Know It *the day of the Brexit vote. Hang in there."*

Figure 4.1 Spotify Brexit advert

> "Dear person who made a playlist called: 'One Night Stand With Jeb Bush Like He's a Bond Girl in a European Casino.' We have so many questions."

Emotion – Different executions in the campaign referenced individual, city-wide, and country-wide moments of emotion, distress, unhappiness, and joy, which they addressed by listening to just the right music.

Energy – Visually, the campaign crackled with energy. From its use of a very un-corporate electric pink and clashing red to iconic images. But also verbally, too, in its encouragement to its users to "Hang in there". Not to mention the campaign's strapline: "Thanks 2016. It's been weird."

Empathy – The whole campaign is about Spotify showing that it understands what its customers are doing and thinking. By knowing which music they're playing at particular moments – on Valentine's Day, on the day of the Brexit vote, and so on – and drawing associations between what was streamed when, the company is showing deep empathy for its customers. After all, the campaign is called "Dear Person", and it doesn't get much more empathetic than that.

Tech Times[4] reported that the idea for the data-driven advertising campaign originated from Spotify's end-of-year, "The Year in Music campaign" in 2015, which showed that user data contained some interesting titbits and insights. According to chief marketing officer Seth Farbman: "That led to the idea of reflecting culture via listener behavior, showing that big data is not depriving marketing of creativity as some have implied. For us, data inspires and gives an insight into the emotion that people are expressing." *Tech Times* dubbed the campaign "the fun side of customer data analytics", and it's certainly that. But it's also a compelling example of data-driven storytelling at its very best.

> **Key takeaway**: The data you collect from your customers can be repurposed to tell data-driven stories that drive engagement through emotion, energy, and empathy.

NOTES

1 http://bit.ly/2d1rZey
2 www.bbc.co.uk/news/uk-37995600
3 http://bit.ly/2shQgnO
4 http://bit.ly/2z1lUZO

5

BEWARE THE CURSE OF KNOWLEDGE

Rather than browbeating the consumer with persuasive messaging which immediately triggers a defence mechanism, storytelling activates neurones that create empathy between the storyteller and the subject.
Lisa Samuels, Health Employees Superannuation Trust of Australia[1]

A DANGEROUS THING

The two core skills that are in highest demand in the data-driven knowledge economy are analytics and storytelling. One: the ability to identify, isolate, and make meaning out of the neighbourhood of little big data that is most relevant to the narrative your organisation seeks to use to differentiate itself. Two: the ability to use the right data, manipulated through clever statistics and set in its proper context, to tell that story in a compelling, coherent, and convincing way. With emotion, energy, and empathy, of course to drive engagement.

Traditionally, it was believed these skills were found in different types of people. Scientists and artists. Introverts and extroverts. Left-brain analysts and right-brain communicators. People who had specialised – and been forced or channelled into specialising by secondary and tertiary education – in one area or another. But the problem with dividing responsibility for these skills into different job functions and roles – to R&D on one side and marketing communications on the other – is that it can be difficult to get these two types of player to play on the same team. Fire and ice can make a spectacular combination, but without a good mediator who can see the middle way between the two, that combination has the potential to end up as just a disappointing puddle of water.

Keeping analytics apart from storytelling and only bringing them together when it's time to tell the story sets organisations up for failure. As generations of Victorian and Edwardian anthropologists and linguists discovered, exploring hidden and pre-industrial societies, if cultures are physically separated, they develop in different ways. They have different forms of society, different cultural conventions, different hierarchical structures, a different pace of working, and, most fundamentally, different modes of communication. They end up speaking a different language. Yes, if they're geographically close it's likely they'll be able to make themselves understood, but words will take on their own meaning and an awful lot will be lost in translation. Both sides can get frustrated and will withdraw if they can't make themselves understood.

The most common complaint that analytics folks have about storytellers is that they dumb the data down. Storytellers don't understand the technical details of what analysts have discovered. They want a one-factor solution when the situation's much more nuanced than that. The stories they look to tell only tell part of the story in a way that trivialises and oversimplifies the very real substance of what they have discovered or developed. Because storytellers lack the technical nous to appreciate the complexity of the analysts' work, the stories they look to build make a mockery of their innovation. Often, analysts see little point in cooperating with the storytellers if all they're going to do is tell the tiny bit of the story that they actually do understand.

On the other side, storytellers often get incredibly frustrated by analysts' inability to explain their findings and their breakthroughs in a simple, clear, and coherent fashion. There are always so many "ifs" and "buts" and "only in certain circumstances". Boffins are supposed to come up with great solutions, aren't they? Not something that we can only claim works with a following wind, every other Thursday, and if there isn't an "r" in the month.

Storytellers absolutely want to build stories with as few interacting factors as possible, because the more factors and contingencies there are to explain, the harder it will be to communicate the benefits of the innovation. It will be harder to engage even specialist, technical media to listen to, write about, and carry the story to those they seek to inform and influence. In the social media world, it will be harder to grab the attention of leading bloggers and those with most reach and influence in the specialist area of the organisation. For organisational storytellers, it can sometimes feel as if analysts are actually working for the opposition.

What this clash of cultures often does is make both sides withdraw and refuse to cooperate and collaborate. It results in more siloed businesses. And most importantly – from this book's perspective – it results in weaker, data-poor stories, rather than impactful, data-driven storytelling.

A TALE OF TEABAG TECHNOLOGY

The first time I saw the walls come down between the analysts and the storytellers was when, in the mid-1990s, I had the privilege to sit on the inside track of one of the most important developments in British culture of the late twentieth century. I talk, of course, of when teabags moved into the third dimension. When PG Tips stole a march on the rest of its competitors by moving from flat and square to three-dimensional and pyramid-shaped. The era of tetrahedral tea was upon us.

As even non-British readers know, tea is an incredibly important part of British culture and British life. Tea is drunk by many Brits all day, every day. The mantle of the nation's biggest tea drinker is hotly disputed between former Labour minister and firebrand Tony Benn – who drank a pint of tea an hour, enough in his lifetime to float the QE2[2] – and the mother of the third and finest Dr Who, Tom Baker – whom Baker claimed in his first autobiography[3] drank up to 72 cups a day.

Not all of us trouble our bladders quite so insistently, but tea is woven into the fabric of British life. It's used to wake us up. As a punctuation point at times of emotional or physical crisis, at both a personal and a national level. Making a cup of tea is an act of kindness and sympathy – "tea and sympathy", after all – and drinking a cuppa makes the world right again, allowing us to put things into perspective. Soap opera features tea being poured almost constantly, although those in soap operas probably need a bit more tea than the average Brit because there's so much going on – and so much tragedy – in the life of your typical EastEnder or Ambridge resident.

When your husband's cheated on you? Time for a cup of tea.

When England are 2–1 down to Iceland in the Euros (you heard me, right)? The national grid goes into meltdown as kettles are flicked on with the half-time whistle.

When another senseless ISIS or Al-Qaida attack brings carnage to the streets of Berlin or Stockholm, but particularly London? The most British expression of how this won't be allowed to disrupt our lives and we'll get on with life as normal, thanks very much, is best manifested through making and sharing a cup of tea.

So, when Unilever decided it needed to make the first major innovation in teabag technology since the introduction of teabags in 1953, they needed to tread carefully. Tampering with tea is like suggesting cricket is played in coloured pyjamas and with a white ball. And Unilever U.K. was particularly cautious at the time because, only a couple of years before, it had relaunched Persil washing powder as Persil Power, and consumer tests showed it eating through and wrecking clothes. The whole innovation had to be scrapped, and it left the CEO nervous and cautious. Unilever had had its Blue Pepsi or New Coke moment. It couldn't afford a misstep with PG Tips.

When I became part of the Project Magic team, I was working for the PR agency that would be launching the new product innovation. Naturally, we were keen to know what the science was behind the innovation. And we were soon introduced to one of the first – and certainly one of the best – data-driven storytellers I've ever come across. He was someone who both set the bar and made me realise early in my career that fire and ice can work together and produce, yes, magic; that telling stories that are underpinned by complex science but don't lead with the equations or workings out really can cut through.

Dr Andrew (Fred) Marquis was a researcher in thermofluids in the Department of Mechanical Engineering at Imperial College, London. He and his colleagues had been briefed by a PG Tips team, including tea tasters and marketers, supply chain and brand managers, to create something truly revolutionary in teabag technology. Something that would improve the brewing experience given by a teabag and make an even better-tasting cuppa.

You see, when you pour boiling water onto a conventional, square, flat teabag, the pressure of the water on the teabag initially squeezes those delicious tannins and flavonoids from the leaves and into the water. But because the teabag is flat, almost as soon as the flow of water stops – when the mug or the teapot is full – teabags tend to clomp up, to use the technical term. The tealeaves stick together and they have no room to move around in the two-dimensional teabag. This reduces the potential for fresh polyphenols to be released from every tealeaf in the teabag, and the brew is suboptimal. To get more taste, people tend to leave the teabag in the cup. But that tends to create a more bitter taste, which some find unpleasant. Or else they grab hold of it and dunk it up and down, and then they usually burn their fingers. The challenge was set.

Rather than dismiss this as marketing fluff or a challenge too trivial, Marquis and his team took up the task with gusto. They dismissed as a mere gimmick the only other innovations in living memory, both as it happens from arch-rival Tetley. The round bag from 1989 was a cute idea (after all, 99% of cups and mugs have round bottoms), but it did nothing to enhance brewing or the taste. And the drawstring bag – designed to squeeze fresh-brewed taste out of teabags relatively early in the brewing process – was incredibly fiddly and liable to snap.

What the Imperial team did was to look to build the first teabag that created and sustained a three-dimensional shape when it floated in the mug or teapot. There were some constraints, of course. It had to be of a shape that could be manufactured by Unilever's teabag-making machines with minimum necessary modification. When teabags are made, the pieces of porous paper are placed either side of the tealeaves and stitched, pressed, or thermo-sealed around them. Also, the finished shape needed to be squishable so it could fit into boxes of a similar size to the 40, 80, and 160-teabag boxes PG Tips made at the time. After all, supermarkets wouldn't suddenly give up twice the space on the shelves just because PG Tips had changed the shape of its teabags, however much better the tea might taste.

What's more, having been squashed, the teabags needed to spring back into shape when boiling water was poured over the top. There would be no chance to introduce a new ritual into the tea-making cere- mony of – say – shaking out the teabag into its 3D shape before popping it into the cup or mug. It needed to perform as intended and improve brewing performance when anyone was making a cuppa, half-asleep, bleary-eyed, or when attending to a domestic or global crisis.

The thermofluids team got to work. They made teabags of every imag- inable three-dimensional shape. They made cubes, spheres, and dodeca- hedrons. And because of the essential Britishness of tea and teabags – and their waggish sense of humour – they also made top hats and bowler hats. But the shape that won out – the shape that could be made using existing machines, that squashed down into boxes but popped back into shape in the mug, and that gave the best brewing performance – was the tetrahedron or four-faced pyramid. It was – as marketing manager Marcus Marsden once observed in an agency meeting – "the teabag that works like a teapot". Thanks very much, said the ad agency, nicking the line for the launch. And pyramid-shaped teabags were born.

Now, the way I tell the story to you is pretty much the way Fred Marquis and his boffins told the story. To the PG Tips technical team. To the Unilever corporate team. To the agencies looking for stories (and coming away with more than they could have hoped for). To Radio 4's *Today Programme* and BBC1's *Tomorrow's World*. Here's Fred[4] talking in *The Independent* in 1996:

> [The pyramid-shaped teabag] tends to naturally float on the surface of the water, allowing the water to flow more freely in and out of the tea bag. It is this extra movement of tea leaves which helps the brewing process.

The teabag that works like a teapot with loose leaf tea.

Of course, there was a wealth of data and statistics underpinning the very complex technology required to produce a tetrahedral teabag.

Thermofluids folks also use a lot of equations. But they kept them for their lab books and computer simulations and the academic papers they published to justify the superior brewing technology the shape provided (academic papers are always a useful weapon in the data-driven storyteller's armoury – though usually a source of weaponry and not the weapon itself). But they had the empathy and the understanding to know who needed to know what, when, and why. Which is why Dr Fred Marquis is the first – and certainly one of the finest – data-driven storytellers I've come across.

Fred was employed as an academic. He was contracted to run an academic research project to fuel a PG Tips product innovation. It was because of his unusually well-developed sense of empathy that he was able to provide the data-driven ammunition Unilever needed to tell a convincing, compelling, evidence-based narrative. He could judge when it was appropriate to be the scientist (with his team and his peers), and when it was appropriate to be the storyteller (with his client and their agencies). Fundamentally, he was able to avoid the Curse of Knowledge.

THE CURSE OF KNOWLEDGE

When you learn about a subject, you know more than most people. It's impossible to unlearn what you've learned (though it is, of course, possible to forget). The more you learn about it, the more expert you become. And yet the more you know, the harder you find it to explain to others who don't know as much as you do. This is called the Curse of Knowledge, and it can have profound effects on how clearly you write or talk about your passion: about your expertise.

In *The Sense of Style*, one of the best books about writing clearly and eloquently, Harvard psychology professor Steven Pinker observes "the more you know, the less clearly you write". Academics often suffer from the Curse of Knowledge, although some display it as a badge of pride, using shortcuts and jargon as a smokescreen to create an exclusive club with a secret language that only the elite few can understand. Fred Marquis didn't do that.

Business writers do it too, particularly – though not exclusively – when they're writing about legal, medical, or technical products or services that are rooted in science. And while science is complicated, explaining the real-world impact of science doesn't need to be. If your product or service or research is as good as you claim it is – if it's going to be helpful or useful to as many people as it possibly could be – you need to talk about it simply and clearly.

Avoiding the Curse of Knowledge comes down to empathy: to understanding that those you're trying to influence – your target audience – don't know as much as about the area where you're expert as you do. Which is why they're coming to you in the first place – because you're an expert and because your product or service can take away their pain. They don't need, and they certainly don't want, to see your workings or hear your rationale.

To avoid the Curse of Knowledge, you need to talk like Apple talks. Talk like Virgin talks. Talk like HSBC talks. To get a very practical sense of what this means, my corporate and brand storytelling business, Insight Agents, scoured the internet to find examples of businesses that fail to avoid the Curse of Knowledge.

In the three examples that follow, we've also scored the language on the Flesch–Kincaid scale for reading ease (see Chapter 2 for more details) to make a second point. Prose that's infected by the Curse of Knowledge is very often hard to read, harder to parse, and hardest yet to understand. This is because it uses technical language that would be more at home in a technical manual, and because it is written without empathy. When organisations write with empathy, they want their audience to understand what they're saying and be as excited by it as they are themselves. They don't want potential supporters, customers, or advocates to be unclear about what they're saying. This is why they put themselves in the shoes of these people – into their minds – and explain themselves clearly and simply. They don't assume knowledge, they assume ignorance.

Consider the case of a business called Regen SW. They describe themselves in this way:[5] "We are an independent not for profit that uses our expertise to work with industry, communities and the public sector to revolutionise the way we generate, supply and use energy." (Flesch Kincaid reading ease score 26.9).

Not the easiest start to a website homepage, and too much information packed into a single sentence. This is particularly true, considering it's the first sentence most first-time visitors will ever read about the business in this, their digital shop window. They're so interested in themselves and their not-for-profit values and the sectors they work with in such a revolutionary way that, what they actually do (energy supply) doesn't feature until word 30 of 30. And that's before they start getting technical with us, and say:

> *Domestic biomass growth indicates degression in April. Forecasting expenditure for biomass is over its degression threshold at the end of November 2014 and therefore requires a 10% degression in April. The question is whether we might see the schemes first 20% degression due to the "super trigger" being hit.*

(FK 44.1)

I've got a bit of a reputation for poking fun at storytelling that's not clear or simple or straightforward to understand, and particularly data-driven storytelling like this. "What does it matter?" victims or fellow sufferers retort. "We're a business to business business, experts selling to other experts. Why shouldn't we talk in the language we talk in day in, day out?"

My simple response is that – of course – "I understand you're experts and brilliant at what you do. That's why other businesses seek you out. You have expertise that they don't and that they need. But because you're the expert and your customers inevitably know less than you, you are doing yourself an active disservice by writing so opaquely. By arrogantly and unempathetically forgetting that everyone doesn't know as much about – and certainly isn't as interested in – your specialist area as you are. You owe it to them to explain it simply and clearly. Simple and clear doesn't mean dumbed down or patronisingly. Shrouding yourself in jargon, being deliberately opaque, and falling foul of the Curse of Knowledge means you are actually limiting the potential you have to grow and succeed as a business."

I really mean that. Poor communication confuses people and they turn off and go and look for a competitor who can explain what they do quicker and simpler. Having words like those picked out above on your home page hamstrings a business. When I make that connection, I've seen hard-nosed sales directors and bolshie heads of R&D go quiet. I often wonder whether the Chief Financial Officer mightn't be a better route to market for a corporate and brand storyteller than the Chief Marketing Officer. I know that econometric modellers find a sympathetic ear from the CFO, because they show the CMO and her marketing teams which half of their advertising budget is wasted. CFOs give that kind of intelligence two thumbs up.

We've already talked a lot about the role of purpose in business. My purpose in running a corporate and brand storytelling business is simple. It's to help companies and brands communicate better, more authentically, more simply. To cut out the jargon, to avoid the Curse of Knowledge, to find and express their purpose, to plan and craft their communication more empathetically. Ultimately – and we'll come to this in Chapter 6 – to talk that rarest of business dialects: Human. My purpose is a simple purpose, but it's one that can have real impact on organisational performance – for-profit or not-for-profit; private or public sector; business, NGO, or charity.

One of the reasons that Simon Sinek's *Start with Why* is the second most-watched TED talk of all time is that he's such a good speaker. It's also because what he says rings so true, and because his message is so simply and elegantly delivered. His thesis is that people don't buy what you do, they buy why you do it. Advice he gives six times in 18 minutes, and it's advice that networking solutions business Zeetta Networks should have considered before they wrote this[6] in the appealing-titled tab on their website called "Our story":

> *Zeetta Networks is a spin-out company from the University of Bristol developing and marketing Open Networking solutions for heterogeneous networks based on Software Defined Networking (SDN) and Network Function Virtualisation (NFV) principles. The company's main product is NetOS®, a Network Operating System which offers a "USB-like",*

plug-n-play management of all connected network devices and enables the construction of virtual "network slices" (i.e. separate logically-isolated sub-networks) for the deployment of B2B or B2C services such as Ultra-HD video distribution, City-wide Wi-Fi, Internet of Things (IoT) and M2M deployments, etc.

(FK 22.3)

By introducing difficult concepts more simply and straightforwardly, these companies could have made their products and services very much easier to understand. But by assuming the readers knew almost as much as the authors, these businesses have made themselves less accessible. Less marketable. And less buyable. They have fallen foul of the Curse of Knowledge.

JARGON MONOXIDE POISONING

For the first dozen years after graduation, I worked in public relations. Each industry I supported had its own jargon, but thanks to the principles drummed into me by my boss-cum-mentor, David Green – an elfin Ulsterman who'd been the news editor of *Farmers Weekly* – I always worked hard to ensure my prose was simple and jargon-free. Whether I was working for the drinks industry, Big Pharma, insurance, or legal services.

When I went back to school in 2000, to study for a master's and then a doctorate in Experimental Psychology, I soon became frustrated by the jargon I had to cut through to understand the areas I was interested in – addiction, memory, and mood. Paper after thesis after presentation was steeped in jargon so deep I concluded the authors didn't want me to grasp what they had found. Everyone seemed to take it as a badge of honour to use language that deliberately excluded outsiders, piling up Latinate, technical terms rather than the earthy Anglo-Saxon I'd come to value so highly. And this from someone whose first degree was in Classics, even if I was always more of a Hellenist than a Latin lover.

After a couple of years, I worked out the reason behind all this jargon. Rather than showing off learning or knowledge, I saw that many academic psychologists I met were trying to confuse their audience and gloss over the fact that their experiments weren't producing the expected results. They coined new terms to cover up the shortcomings of their research. Worst of all, they were actively looking to keep others out who weren't part of their club, their tribe, their niche.

Social psychology observes the same about the origins and purpose of street slang and argot, pidgins, and creoles. They're about communication – and effective communication – but only between those in the know. Language can be a powerful tool in building in-groups and out-groups. But in the world of organisational storytelling – particularly storytelling fuelled by data and statistics – those telling the stories should work hard to see that jargon has no place. One of the original Mad Men, David Ogilvy, said: "Our business is infested with idiots who try to impress by using pretentious jargon." What was a problem in 1940s Madison Avenue remains a problem in twenty-teens cyberspace.

When I returned from academia to commercial communications, I vowed to take three things with me: an ability to read, understand, and communicate simply what a research paper really means; a facility with statistics, which has since evolved into data-driven storytelling; and a total rejection of jargon wherever possible: jargon – the smokescreen of the insecure.

Ever since the year 2000, the U.K. Society for Storytelling has run an event called National Storytelling Week, which it uses to run events across the country to promote the oral tradition of storytelling. My business, Insight Agents, supports this event each year. In 2016, we commissioned the University of Sussex to talk to a cross-section of marketing professionals about what they thought about jargon. We found, perhaps unsurprisingly, that they didn't like it.

We also found a very real sense that corporate structures often make jargon inevitable. Modern business is increasingly complicated and technical, and innovations to shout about are often about the marginal gains added in the lab or by finance. Our interviewees said that those who generate really meaningful innovations often don't want their advances dumbed down or explained away in simple terms. If only they could have met or recruited Dr Fred Marquis.

Our research concluded that some marketing and communications folk, whose job it is to tell their corporations' stories, can be prevented from getting to the simple truth of what's new. As a result, too often the advances companies make lay buried beneath a mountain of jargon. They fail to have the galvanic impact they could on corporate reputation and performance. Counter-intuitively – our University of Sussex researchers found – the more complex and technical a business is, the more prepared R&D are to allow a straightforward story to be told.

Kathy Klotz-Guest is a marketing storyteller and founder of Keeping It Human, a firm whose mission is to help companies turn marketing-speak into compelling, authentic, human stories for customers and employees to act on. Sound familiar? Kathy's coined the brilliant phrase "jargon monoxide", reasoning: "Jargon is more than just lazy; it's marketing air pollution." Common as it can be in corporate and marketing speak of any organisation, it's also commonly found in scientific, biomedical, and particularly academic circles. The relatively recent requirement for researchers to report on and articulate the real world impact their research has outside of academia is changing this, but change is slow.

I finished and presented my doctoral research in a month under three years, and its key finding was this: people repeatedly binge on booze because they fail to learn from the bad things that happen to them when they get drunk. Quite simple, no? I could bore you for hours about the experimental manipulations I ran, about the well-validated stimuli I used to create a lab environment that best mimicked a naturalistic drinking environment, or about the multivariate analysis of variance tests I used to analyse the more complex data sets. Indeed, I reckon as many as 70,000 of 125,000 words in my thesis are in the results sections. But you'd by fast asleep before you got to the second chapter.

As a storyteller, the best moment of my viva defence – and perhaps the highpoint of my PhD – was when my two examiners said: "Before we start, can we congratulate you on the most jargon-free thesis we've ever read?" Over a drink to celebrate, they reckoned they'd examined 120 doctoral theses between them. I'm not claiming it's a page-turner, but I'm delighted it was relatively jargon-free. And, therefore, a good read.

Some of those marketers our Sussex researchers spoke to in our National Storytelling Week research said they used jargon in order to demonstrate their expertise and develop trust with consumers. Former president of Yale, Kingman Brewster, Junior, said that: "Incomprehensible jargon is the hallmark of a profession". Experience says this is true, but we also know that while jargon may demonstrate expertise, it erodes trust in organisational storytelling.

THE STORYTELLERS OF TODAY AND TOMORROW

The twin forces of Big Data and social media are changing the way that more and more people are working in the knowledge economy.

The mass availability of data means that many more people have access to – and need to interrogate and tame – data with statistics in order to thrive in their jobs. If they're going to convince people inside and outside their organisations to take a particular course of action – if they're going to effectively move them to change their behaviour – they have really powerful tools at their disposal to help build an effective, evidence-based narrative.

Social media has transformed organisations. They have moved from narrow, command-and-control operations where communication with external stakeholders is performed by a very select few to much more free-form organisations where many more voices matter. Traditionally structured and siloed organisations may kick against this, but their people are voicing opinions on Twitter and LinkedIn and elsewhere outside the organisation's direct control. And where many more voices matter – where organisational dialogue has been replaced forever by much more of a two-way street – storytelling becomes part of everyone's responsibility.

In this new environment, earmarking and restricting skillsets into particular individuals and departments no longer makes sense.

Yes, businesses will always need R&D departments to research and develop the next generation of products and services. But we need R&D

people to develop more storytelling skills to shape the data and statistics that underpin their innovations into compelling, convincing narratives.

Yes, organisations will always need communications departments to be the official conduit of communication between the organisation and its publics. But marcomms people need to enhance their analytics skills to harness the potential that data and statistics provide for better, more impactful, evidence-based storytelling.

What's more, I have already seen a model in which the communications or marketing (or marketing communications) department of an organisation plays much more of an advisory or facilitative role than one that insists all communications must flow through it and it alone. Working with the thought leaders in the organisation, they prepare powerful, compelling, emotional content that its people are then empowered to use. Marcomms distribute so-called Bills Of Marketing (or BOMs) to anyone who might interact with any of the organisation's external stakeholders. These BOMs contain content on the same theme, delivered – say – in a long-form white paper, a blog post, 50-word summaries for LinkedIn, quotes from thought leaders, tweets, killer stats, facts, and soundbites. Those so empowered then pick and choose the content they need – in the format and length they need it – and get communicating. It's like Blair, Mandelson, and the new Labour pledge card – only more so.

Where this brave new, mashed-up world is going to have to run fastest is in skills development.

Those with more outward facing roles need training in analytics – in searching for, finding, and distilling great stories in data.

Those with more inward-facing, analytical, R&D-type roles need training in storytelling – how to use the data and statistics with which they're more familiar to tell better, more human, more emotional stories. Stories that truly move people to take action. Stories that make the organisation come alive in the minds and imaginations of those it seeks to influence.

Training is one approach. Job shares and job swaps are two more. And one that I'm just beginning to hear about involves R&D sending analytics ambassadors to regular marketing communications meetings, and marketing communications returning the favour to R&D. Cross-collaboration can even be brought about by simple mechanics like the compulsory morning coffee and afternoon tea sessions that organisations such as the Medical Research Council's psychology faculty at Cambridge imposed on its members – however senior – some decades ago. The only excuse for non-attendance there is being out of the building or running an experiment.

The new world of organisational storytelling doesn't demand that everyone performs exactly the same function in their jobs. Some will always be more interested and able to craft narrative, while others will always be more at home with data and statistics. But what this hybrid approach should ensure is that everyone knows more about why the organisation exists and what makes it different; they should be able to use the data generated by the organisation to build the foundations of great stories; finally, they should be able to craft and tell these stories. Organisations should therefore feel like they're working towards a common purpose, and those many more voices that matter are much more likely to be on-message.

SUMMING UP

Analytics and storytelling are the defining skills required by increasing numbers of players in the knowledge economy.

Both disciplines need to merge and speak one another's language.

Australian health educator Lisa Samuels is right when she says those in the influence game shouldn't try to browbeat others into accepting a new way of thinking. That just leads to an entrenched defence response and rejection.

Historically, analytical types believe storytellers dumb down their data and statistics, while storytellers get frustrated by analysts' inability to express their breakthroughs clearly.

The story of how researchers at Imperial College developed the PG Tips pyramid teabag is a case study in how to build a great data-driven story.

Being an expert on a subject has one major negative to it: the Curse of Knowledge.

The Curse of Knowledge dictates that the more you know, the less clearly you tend to write and speak. It is impossible to unlearn expertise.

What matters in data-driven storytelling is to wear your learning lightly and explain clearly and straightforwardly.

The Curse of Knowledge reveals a lack of empathy on the part of the storyteller.

Shrouding an organisational story in jargon makes it very much less likely that the organisation will succeed to its full potential.

Writing infected with the Curse of Knowledge drives potential collaborators, advocates, and customers into the arms of competitors who take more care over their storytelling.

Jargon is a smokescreen put up the insecure to keep others out. It should be avoided at all costs, particularly when telling stories with data and statistics.

Jargon erodes trust in organisational storytelling.

Big Data and social media mean analysts need to become better storytellers and storytellers better analysts.

It's not that everyone needs to do the same jobs, but training, job swaps, and ambassadors from analytics to storytelling – from R&D to marketing communications – and back again can help make organisations work better together. Everyone understands their purpose.

Rather than insist on doing all the talking, progressive marketing communications functions now provide everyone in an organisation with Bills Of Marketing which all those empowered can use for dialogue with external stakeholders and media in the right format for them.

GIVE IT A GO: THE KILLER STAT

What is the single most important data point that defines and characterises your organisation? Look at the favourite and current data that your organisation puts out into the public domain. On your website. In your news releases. In your blogs and social media.

Do you believe that your organisation is an effective data-driven storyteller? Does it lead with data? Does it use just the right amount of data or far too much? How would you change your organisation's data-driven storytelling strategy?

When you've found the killer stat, start socialising and sharing it with colleagues. And see how long it is before the information comes back to you.

DATA-DRIVEN STORIES

The safest driver

What's the organisation? AVIVA	
What's the brand? Car insurance	
What's the campaign? The safest driver	
What's the story? AVIVA used an app-based game to motivate customers to make their driving behaviour better and safer.	
How did data drive the story? The app captured actual driving data of thousands who participated, enabling AVIVA to rate and rank those family/friendship groups who took part in the challenge, report on trends among different types of drivers, and better inform their own policy teams on how their drivers actually behaved on the road.	
What was the outcome of the campaign? Thought leadership in the area of road safety, active engagement with a low consideration category, validating the premium for AVIVA branded insurance.	

Insurance is a low interest category, and motor insurance is a low interest product. It's viewed by most as a necessary evil, something that has to be sorted out and paid for. Once it's sorted, it's generally ignored until just around renewal time. The only age groups for whom it's a high interest category and product are the young – particularly young men – aged 17–25, for whom insurance premiums are punishingly expensive. This is because young men are likely to drive faster, take more risks, have more accidents . . . and so make more claims. Oh, and the parents of young drivers – particularly young men – who are often required to make a partial or full contribution to the cost of these sky-high insurance premiums.

Interest in the insurance category has been hijacked over the past ten years by the advent and the flourishing of price comparison websites (PCWs): companies in the U.K. such as Go Compare, Compare the Market (Meerkat), and Confused.com. Fierce competition among the PCWs – including some of the biggest TV and digital search budgets of any advertisers in the country – has effectively commoditised the insurance market, making price almost the only point of differentiation in a saturated marketplace. Most motor insurance policies are bought after research and often instant redirection from PCWs.

This has brought the role of branding in insurance companies into question. Of course, it's important for insurance companies to have name awareness and brand recognition for when their names appear on PCWs' aggregated insurance deals. It's not every customer – not even desperate young men – who buy on price and price alone. Brand value and stature still count in the category – particularly for those brands that refuse to sell via the PCWs – even if it's low interest. But the PCWs have not only commoditised the market. In so doing, they have given branded insurance businesses an existential crisis.

The branded insurers have started to fight back. AVIVA has shaken off and at the same time capitalised on a slightly fusty, paternalistic mantle of "insurer knows best" to morph into a much more active, sage brand that is synonymous with encouraging and rewarding safer driving. And it's done that in no small part through a multi-channel, data-driven storytelling campaign.

In early 2016 – always a noisy time of year for the insurance industry, after the complete turn-off of the month around Christmas – AVIVA launched a new, integrated campaign called the AVIVA Drive Challenge. A first TV commercial introduced us to the Joliffe–Austin family from Newport, who were among the first to take up the challenge (hint – why don't you, too?). This was accompanied by content delivered through social media sites, including Facebook, YouTube, and Twitter.

The minute-long ad told the story of how the Joliffe–Austins were going head-to-head to see who was the safest driver in their family, using

the AVIVA drive app (hint – why don't you download it?). In a brief 60 sec-
onds, we were exposed to gender and age stereotypes found in this – and
probably many other – families about who would be the better driver.
The kids, the parents, or the grandparents. The men or the women. The
cautious or the devil-may-care.

The app measures driving for 200 miles and then gives a safe driving
score out of ten based on cornering, braking, and acceleration. What's
so smart about this data-driven storytelling campaign is the way AVIVA is
motivating drivers to take interest in the issue of driving more safely – and
interest in AVIVA – by turning safer driving into a game. The opportunity
to set up a competition with family and friends is clever and humanises
the initiative, but there's actually no need to run a competition alongside
anyone else. AVIVA says explicitly on its website in promoting downloads
of its app that it expects that 40% of drivers who score 7.1 or more out of
10 will receive an average of £170 a year or more off comprehensive car
insurance with AVIVA.

What's also smart about this campaign is that it uses the data and
statistics that AVIVA can capture from the telematics app to deliver direct
savings to its customers. By incentivising better driving performance in
order to benefit from reduced insurance costs, customers are required to
continue driving safely in order to continue to benefit from the insurance
savings.

But AVIVA isn't only interested in sourcing customer driving performance data to reward those whose driving behaviour merits reduced
premiums. By having thousands of drivers using its app, drivers who are
required to register the demographic profiles against their unique iden-
tifier and device, AVIVA is able to get a picture of how different types
of driver are driving without having to go to the expense of installing
costly black boxes in their drivers' vehicles. The motion sensors and
GPS tracking systems built in to smartphones do away with the need for
any AVIVA-funded hardware. The hardware has already been bought by
AVIVA's customers and app users in the form of their smartphones.

The data can be used for all sorts of purposes, including those related
to data-driven storytelling. AVIVA can use it to highlight who – not just
in each family but also in each TV region or city, with sufficient people

using the app – is the safest type of driver. And who the least safe. By aggregating results on a regional and national level, AVIVA's policy and premium setting departments can have access to more, better, and more up-to-date data about those driving while covered by AVIVA than ever before. And since all of this data will of necessity be anonymised, there's no danger for individual drivers that personally identifiable (aka PII) data with their name attached will go missing or be handed to any other third parties.

All in all, participation in the AVIVA Driver Challenge is a small price to price to pay for cheaper car insurance, safer driving, and a warm feeling about a branded insurance business who'd been pretty low down on the interest or consideration list for many years before.

NOTES

1 http://bit.ly/2j071nx
2 http://huff.to/2nZwXwo
3 *Who on Earth Is Tom Baker? – An Autobiography* (1998). HarperCollins.
4 http://ind.pn/2omnQYJ
5 http://bit.ly/2oUjTxA
6 www.zeetta.com/our-story/

6

TALK HUMAN

We're all in sales, and selling isn't just selling . . . we need to consider sales in a broader sense – persuading, influencing and convincing others.
Daniel Pink (2013), *To Sell is Human*

FUSTIAN FLUMMERY AND FLAPDOODLE

It's a strange truism of corporate communications that, as soon as they're required to write "for" or "as" an organisation, perfectly eloquent individuals often adopt a register that's never come out of any human mouth. It's as if being thrust in the spotlight paralyses usually clear and lucid people to start talking gobbledygook and poppycock, balderdash and baloney, and all manner of other nonsense so beautifully captured here by the online glossary from Phronistery.[1]

---

ackamarackus – baboonery – balderdash – ballyhoo – baloney – bambosh – bilge – blague – blarney – bletherskate – brimborion – bugaboo – buncombe – bunk – bushwa – cack – claptrap – clatfart – codswallop – effutiation – eyewash – fadoodle – falderal – fandangle – fiddlededee – fiddle-faddle – flam – flannel – flapdoodle – flimflam – flummadiddle – flummery – fribble – fustian – galbanum – galimatias – gammon – gibberish –

grimgribber – haver – hibber-gibber – hogwash – hooey –
humbug – jabberwock – jiggery-pokery – kilter – kidology –
linsey-woolsey – macaroni – malarkey – morology – mullock –
mumbo-jumbo – narrischkeit – nugament – phonus-bolonus –
piddle – pigwash – poppycock – posh – quatsch – rannygazoo –
razzmatazz – rhubarb – riddle-me-ree – rottack – schmegeggy –
shuck – skittles – slipslop – spinach – squit – stultiloquence –
taradiddle – tarradiddle – tootle – tosh – trumpery – twaddle

When English is such a powerful, varied, colourful tool as this, how is it that the function of organisational storytelling renders people so hopelessly and helplessly unable to use language for its primary purpose: to communicate and convey complex and often abstract concepts clearly and succinctly? This challenge is often especially acute for those who use data and statistics as the foundation of their organisational storytelling. Let's consider now some of the reasons why corporate speak often misses the mark and some ways you can ensure your statements can be expressed rather less stultiloquently.

Psychology – For many people, speaking or presenting to an audience brings them out in cold sweat. They feel naked – or they'd rather walk through their workplace naked than have to stand up and talk to their peers or colleagues, to internal or external stakeholders. This fear extends to writing about their organisation too, even when they have time and checks and balances, others to assess and improve their copy. The very act of being asked to commit something to words deprives some people of the ability to do what's come naturally to them since they first absorbed the language around them as infants.

> *Top tips: If you're writing for a tweet or a post or a blog or a webpage or a paper, speak out loud what you write. Does it sound human? Would you understand it if you heard it?*

Time pressure – Corporate spokespeople are often under immense time pressure, from journalists and bloggers, bosses and colleagues, to create copy and content. It might be in response to specific questions. It might be because of publication deadlines. It might be because a colleague is unexpectedly absent and the task has been dropped on you. It might be because, if you can't provide an answer, the person demanding content will go elsewhere – to a competitor or a rival. These pressures are significantly increased in our social and digital media world, where the timely response to a hostile tweet could snuff out a story and stop it in its tracks, whereas a tardy one could add fuel to the flames of a crisis.

Perversely, time pressure can also force people to write more words than if they're allowed more time to write the right words. More words, but often much, much less clarity. As Winston Churchill, Mark Twain, and Oscar Wilde are all said to have said: "I would have written you a shorter letter, but I didn't have the time."

> *Top tips: Establish the absolute priority of the request for copy, comment, or content as soon as you receive it. Give in to the tyranny of the urgent over the important until you've dealt with what really matters.*

Projected norms – Partly through observing how companies/politicians/organisations often talk, partly through caricature and satire, and partly because communication has traditionally been a function performed by a limited number of people in an organisation, there is a projected norm about what corporate-speak should be like. A folk memory representation, if you like. While this is changing through the speed of social media and the fact that many more voices matter, the caricature of corporate-speak lingers on.

The projected norm of corporate-speak is a little awkward and stultified. It comes from the mouths of suits, happy to use long words and longer sentences to deliver a message that says effectively nothing. The fact that more and more people are thrust and are thrusting themselves into the spotlight through social channels and platforms is having a positive impact on corporate-speak. It is also helping to correct the often-erroneous projected norms of organisational storytelling. Both have become more quickfire and casual – human, not slapdash.

> *Top tips: Learn from what a company active and effective on Twitter says through there, more than what it says in its annual report. That said, those organisations that have truly mastered how to talk human can do so in every channel and medium at their disposal.*

Organisational structure – By this I don't mean silos and departments – although these can often be the origin of corporate multiple personality disorder and different – sometimes conflicting or competing – voices. No, rather I mean that organisations are abstract concepts, with rules and governance, norms, and conventions. However, fundamentally any organisation – a company, an academic department, an NGO or charity – is a collection of humans working together for a common purpose. Yes, what they do may well be powered to a greater or lesser extent by technology; Spotify depends more on tech to deliver what it does than the Royal Society of Arts, but they would both be nothing without their people. And people achieve things by persuading other people to follow them – by moving them through evidence-based, emotional appeals.

> *Top tips: Realise that, however tech-rich and data-driven, all organisations are populated by people and that people make the decisions. They may be guided by data and statistics, but no decision will be made without the guiding hand of purpose and motivation. So, use arguments that appeal to people – human-to-human – balancing evidence with emotion and empathy. Algorithms matter, but not as much as humanity.*

Fear of unintended consequences – Responding in the right or the wrong way can have profound, career-limiting consequences. Say or write the wrong thing to the wrong person or on the wrong platform, and you can send the company share price tumbling or get your organisation into legal hot water. In these circumstances, there are a couple of tendencies to watch out for. Saying too much is easy. You're asked for one figure or one statistic, and you give a mountain in response. You think you're being helpful, but you're throwing bad data after good. Rather than using simple, straightforward language, you lapse into jargon and the curious register of corporate-speak, piling abstract noun onto technical term. In fact, you're helping no one and sounding more stupid by the moment. Stop.

> Top tips: Say what you need to and no more. Learn to love the sound of silence. Don't throw fuel on the fire by saying more and more when you've already answered the question.

Poor planning – When you're looking to control the flow of information, particularly through 24/7 cycle of news and social media, you need to realise that your organisation's point of view will very rarely be the only or dominant perspective to govern the story that is ultimately told. This is true, even if the story starts with a crisis (or an incredible success) driven by what your organisation has said or done. There will be competitors and peers, regulatory authorities, representative and/or trade bodies, politicians, academics, and all manner of other stakeholders who can make the story better or different or carry on burning.

> Top tips: Even in the eye of a crisis, take time out to plan what you're going to say. Be empathetic enough to understand what others want and need from you, and don't throw numbers or factoids at the problem – about how you're doing brilliantly everywhere other than where there's a crisis, say – to try to divert attention. Consider the impact of every response you may make, and check with a member of your team whether what you're about to say sounds authentic and human.

Jargon – We considered the impact of the Curse of Knowledge in detail in Chapter 5. This phenomenon – which makes it hard to explain simply something you know in detail – very often makes organisational storytellers sound like they're speaking another language. They use technical details and jargon as if everyone should understand them. They liberally sprinkle data and statistics through their conversation or copy because surely anyone can see how relevant they are, how they build the story up.

> *Top tips: Strip out the jargon. Assume no knowledge of your specialist area. Use data and statistics as the rationale and the underpinning of the story you're telling, but never lead with them or use them as the story. Evidence-based narrative is more effective and impactful than organisational stories that are based on thin or hot air. But it's the presence of data in the background, data that can be brought forward on request if the questioner is interested and asks, "Tell me more . . .", that matters. Not grandstanding or talking like you're trying to browbeat another into submission with numbers, numbers, numbers. Though you can allow yourself one killer number or stat to lead off a story, provided it truly is that.*

The language of statistics – One of the joys of data and statistics is that they are an incredibly dense and compact way of telling stories. There's an awful lot packed into numbers that have been crunched down from millions or billions of rows of data. But beware. Statistics comes with its own jargon and shorthand, and it's a dialect that many either don't understand or wilfully choose to ignore. This can be dangerous. For example, even some science and medical writers on leading news outlets have little or no understanding or respect for the concepts of relative and absolute risk. The term "statistically significant" is very often confused with the non-specialist word "significant". Why else would the *Daily Mail* routinely flip and flop between "caffeine causes cancer" and "caffeine cures cancer" in its health news reporting? What other explanation is there for the long run that struck-off doctor Andrew Wakefield was given when he tried to connect the MMR vaccine to autism?

> *Top tips: Follow the guidance issued and the principles set out by Sense About Science (http://senseaboutscience.org) in reporting*

scientific news, data, and research. Be judicious about how you present research findings or analytics. When reporting health, drug trial, and environmental impact data, make sure that it isn't open to wilful misinterpretation, particularly the "significance" of the findings. If one family member has been made ill by a fast-food outlet's hygiene standards, that's a story (and very "significant" to them). But if – in response – a corporate spokesperson gives raw data or expected numbers of infections from e-coli or salmonella when they're serving millions of meals a day, that's a full-blown crisis and a tumbling share price. Be judicious and empathetic.

B2B, B2C, OR SOMETHING ELSE ALTOGETHER?

Consumer-facing businesses and brands clearly understand the importance of talking with a human voice to their customers: of talking like one person to another. Many consumer brands have clearly defined personalities, often derived from Jungian archetypes – though that's another (and someone else's) story. The human voice has long been used by consumer brands – so-called business-to-consumer or B2C – for communications intended to reach customers directly, through advertising, public relations activity, and, increasingly, social media. When it's done right, the company or brand speaks with a single, coherent voice which is instantly recognisable. Apple, easyJet, and Disney are all good examples for B2C done human.

Speaking directly to consumers about consumery things is one aspect of effective B2C communication. In parallel with the advent and growth of social, many B2C businesses and brands have learned to expand their ability to talk human across all of their communication, dealing with all external stakeholder groups. This includes in their investor relations (dealing with investors, analysts, and the City), in their public affairs (dealing with legislators and regulators), and in their professional communications (dealing with partner businesses, trade customers, and trade associations).

In many cases, a B2C business communicating to external stakeholder groups apart from their customers have to communicate complex, technical, data-rich information, informed by research and analytics. Those that do this best use the same human voice, the same register as they do for their direct-to-consumer communication. Many B2C businesses have identified and expressed their purpose, and increasingly they follow Simon Sinek's advice and start with "Why?"

Business-to-business or B2B communication has always lagged behind B2C in its willingness and ability to talk human. B2B has been the poor relation of B2C. The justification (or excuse) has been that B2B businesses are talking about more technical or complicated issues than B2C and so they can't use such simple (or dumbed down) language as their brighter, more sparkly cousins. The same excuse is made by many academics, professional services firms (lawyers, accountants, consultants – but particularly lawyers), politicians, bureaucrats, civil servants, and regulators. They're dealing with difficult stuff and complex arguments, often full of in-depth statistical analysis of multivariate data sets. So, how can they possibly use language as basic and pared back as B2C brands to make their case? They lapse into jargon without any provocation – claiming it's a shorthand that saves time, when in fact it's just keeping non-experts (often the very businesses they're dealing with) out of a comprehensive understanding of what they're trying to say.

Jargon gets in the way when representatives of an organisation talk to one audience but another audience inadvertently overhears what they've said. This is almost inevitable in our social media world, where it's next to impossible to prevent corporate speak aimed at shareholders from being overheard by the general public. And it's why companies should try wherever possible to speak with one voice, to tell one, true, authentic story, not multiple versions in different registers.

For CEOs, lapsing into jargon reveals a fundamental disconnect between the boardroom and their employees and customers. Just consider Tesco CEO Dave Lewis, who recently praised the company's "customercentricity" (all one word, in spoken and written form); poor form from a struggling CEO in a struggling business which has been accused of routinely failing to put its customers first in recent years. Much worse, though, was when United Airlines' Oscar Muñoz spoke after a passenger had been dragged off a plane in spring 2017. He talked about "reaccommodating" and "deplaning" a "disruptive and belligerent passenger". He maintained that his staff were "following established procedures". That feels painfully close to "we were only obeying orders".

Let's take another example – current at time of writing, and doubtless current for many years to come: the effectiveness of online advertising. In the second half of 2016 and the first half of 2017, evidence has been mounting that online advertising is delivering very poor return on investment. This is for reasons of fraud (advertisers paying for ads that never appear), poor viewability (ads "seen" only by bots and not humans, or not at all), and brand safety (ads being placed programmatically by algorithms in unsafe environments). As a result, the global digital advertising industry is falling over itself to put its rotten house in order. Google, Facebook, YouTube, and Twitter – the main beneficiaries of boom in online advertising – have made statements and issued ads aimed at reassuring other businesses that their platforms are safe and effective and worth continuing to invest in.

Yet, because the problems have been in existence for many years and have been talked about at industry conferences for almost as long, these protestations and reassurances ring a little hollow. Particularly when they're endlessly caveated by "we are just the medium, not the message", and "we don't say who can say what, we just provide the technology to enable sharing of all the amazing creativity on the planet". All the amazing creativity like ISIS and Al-Qaida, like extreme right racist hate groups, like paedophiles and abusive pornographers.

These platforms have missed a trick. Their businesses ooze data. Google's very purpose is to organise the world's information (not a bad one, though not always perfectly realised). They have it within their gift to use their user and advertising data and a frank and comprehensive analysis of that data as the basis for a powerful piece of organisational storytelling. To date, they've not taken up that challenge. Certainly, not nearly as impactfully as music streaming platform Spotify did, as shown in Figure 6.1.

Figure 6.1 Spotify business ad
Hitting the high notes: Spotify's data-driven story to reassure advertisers during the heat of the 2017 digital advertising crisis

This ad is simple, frank, and informative. It acknowledges the very real difficulties of the environment and the very real concerns advertisers have about fraud, safety, and effectiveness. Yes, it uses a sprinkling of technical language. That's justifiable, because it's addressing a technical audience.

But it doesn't go over the top, and it doesn't make its prose unreadable or incomprehensible, and least of all inauthentic to a lay reader. What's more, it uses light-touch data and statistics to reinforce key messages. Full marks, Spotify.

Complexity and difficulty are not reasons or justifications. They're just excuses. As we saw with Dr Fred Marquis. As we've seen with This Girl Can and Tesco and AVIVA. It's perfectly possible to talk human and still incorporate complex data and statistics as the fundamental underpinning of your organisational storytelling. It's perfectly possible to make direct and emotional appeals, from one human to another, whoever's talking and whoever's listening. Not only is it perfectly possible, but it's also demonstrably more effective and impactful.

This is why business consultant and TED Talker Bryan Kramer has gone so far as to say, "There is no B2B or B2C: it's human to human, #H2H." This makes perfect sense. As we saw in the introduction, humans are hardwired to respond to stories and to story structure. The three-act story with a beginning, a middle, and an end, first set out in Aristotle's *Poetics*. The 12-stage hero's journey, that underpins so much of what is great and works so well in literature and films and epic TV series.

Using the principles of great storytelling – telling real stories about real people, which use evidence and facts and statistics as their foundation but not as the stories themselves – organisations of whatever type can succeed in Dan Pink's "moving business". They can lay out the reasons, supported by emotion, of why their target audience should listen to them. Should support them. Should go on to become their advocates. Or reject them altogether. But better to get a strong reaction than a bland "Meh?" or a look of total incomprehension because your organisation failed to realise the power and the value of communicating human-to-human.

KNOW YOUR AUDIENCE

It's been a dictum for storytellers from the beginnings of the oral tradition onwards that to tell a good story, you really have to know your audience. What are they looking to get out of the stories you're telling and therefore (a) how should you address them – including what type of language should you use – and (b) and what should your stories be about?

Popularity alone is no absolute indicator that your stories are having the desired effect. Yes, it's a good marker of interest if theatres are packed out. If your audience share is the highest on record. If night after night a crowd of several hundred gather round you in the Jemaa el-Fnaa on the edge of the souk in Marrakech. Yet you may only want to address a small and very specific audience, in which case a large audience would be likely to include many whom you're not seeking to influence or address. It's not – necessarily – that you don't want them to hear your message, it's just that they're not the people you and your organisation are seeking to move or motivate to action.

Knowing your audience comes down – yet again – to empathy. One of the golden threads running through this book is how organisational storytellers can use data and statistics as the foundation for better, more impactful stories. But underpinning a lot of the rules and principles of data-driven storytelling comes empathy: the ability to put yourself in your audience's shoes and see the world from their point of view. This requires what developmental psychologists call a theory of mind, and it is the facility that researchers have shown is often faulty or missing from those on the autistic spectrum, and why one of the definitions or descriptions of the condition is sometimes "mind blindness".

Empathy requires a storyteller to put themselves in the position of the individual or individuals she is trying to influence and wonder what it would be like to hear the story she plans to tell. How much detail do they want? What should the balance be between fact and rhetoric? How should I use emotion? What's the role for data and statistics? Should I show my workings out? Am I confident I know how I got to the answer I'm sharing? Could I justify my thinking if pressed?

To be candid, empathy is a – the – fundamental human quality that underpins brilliant storytelling. At least for humans who don't also happen to be psychopaths. Psychopaths tend to feel no or very little empathy, which is why they find it easy to inflict mental or physical pain, to steal from or torture others. This is because they are actually unable to transpose their mental state into what it must be like to be the victim of the abuses to which they put their victims. But psychopathy is someone else's story (and Jon Ronson's written a very good one).

The number of humans who can and who do tell stories on behalf of organisations is spreading, thanks to the exponential growth of Big Data and the ready availability of social media tools and platforms. Humans telling stories that they want to be effective – an obvious purpose, for otherwise, why bother? – need to max out their empathy radar and really get under the skin of those they're trying to influence. With the audience in mind, they can much more easily judge the role that data and statistics can and should play in the totality of their tale. As I've said several times in this book, data and statistics are readily available and really matter, but they matter much more as the underpinning and the foundations of an organisational story than they do as the story itself. Being empathetic is all about observing the principles of the Cocktail Party Rule.

THE COCKTAIL PARTY RULE

Bear with me just a little while for this *Mad Men* – era analogy. I do appreciate that cocktail parties aren't either as frequent or as popular as they were. I understand that society has moved on, in the types of gathering that are popular and in the form and formats of psychotropic drugs that lubricate many different types of social interaction – including the increasingly popular "no drugs at all".

But there's something beguiling about the cocktail party era, and particularly about those who shone and captured others' attention at these events. Yes, of course, the attractive and the powerful and the influential would always attract a crowd. But why – apart from high cheek bones and buxom figures, well-filled suits and cocktail dresses – did those who drew the crowds manage to do so? It certainly wasn't always because they were matinée idols.

In no small part, the reason that some cocktail party guests rather than others draw attention and gather a crowd is because they think before they even enter the building about the audience they'll talking to. As they enter the room, they may need to adjust their empathy radar, based on which individuals and what type of people are present. Some they will know, but most they will not, and they'll have to quickly judge the mood of the room and the guests to know what they should talk about. For the Cocktail Party Rule states:

> **If you want to be boring, talk about yourself. If you want to be interesting, talk about what matters to those who are listening.**

Talk about what those you want to impress, to influence – to become your friends and advocates – are interested in. Or else run the risk of being the bore talking to themselves in the corner at the end of the evening.

The Cocktail Party Rule applies every bit as much to a 1950s-cocktail party as it does to organisational storytelling in the late twenty-teens. It has particular resonance for how you choose to use data and statistics as a core foundation of your storytelling, but not as the story itself. Imagine how quickly your audience at a cocktail party would scuttle away like cockroaches if you started to list off a reel of statistics to try to make your point; if you used no emotion in your language; if you didn't follow the three-act structure in your anecdotes.

Being empathetic, talking human, and making judicious use of data and statistics to build your story are all driven by knowing your audience. When you sit down to write – a speech, a tweet, a blog, or a white paper – try to imagine the individuals in your target audience around you as if you were at a cocktail party, Don Draper and Betty Olson on the fringes of your group. And see if you can't keep them hanging on your every word, rather than slipping quietly away to engage with someone less boring instead. Hear the Cocktail Party Rule as you plan and write. Maybe even print it out and stick it on your office wall. "If you want to be boring . . ."

One final point. The Cocktail Party Rule is one of the reasons that organisations creating content about issues not themselves – so-called content marketing – has grown to be so popular and so successful; why white papers about industry issues are downloaded so much more frequently than corporate brochures or product information sheets. Once they're aware of who you are and what you do, potential customers and collaborators have no doubt that there are things you could do for them. But rather than hear how wonderful you are or how many offices you have or what your revenue in their sector was last year, they'd much rather know what you think about the issues that are plaguing their sector today.

When you talk about the issues that matter to those who are listening, you'll soon draw a surprisingly big and engaged crowd. All because of the power of the Cocktail Party Rule.

WHAT TALKING HUMAN SOUNDS LIKE

It makes sense to round out this chapter – and the theory and advice section of the book – with some examples of what talking human sounds like. However soft, calm, and conversational HAL 9000 was in Stanley Kubrik's film of Arthur C. Clarke's *2001: A Space Odyssey*, he – it – was still a **H**euristically programmed **AL**gorithmic computer, totally reliant on code. However convincing the pioneering ELIZA was at asking low-level psychiatric questions, she was still an early natural language processing program developed in the 1960s at MIT, totally reliant on analytics. And however depressed Marvin the Paranoid Android was in Douglas Adams' five-part *Hitchhiker's Guide to the Galaxy* trilogy, he was totally reliant on circuits that fizzed with humanoid-made algorithms.

The advances in language processing and comprehension have made great strides in recent years. IBM's Watson is an extraordinary corpus of programming that can do truly amazing things with language. Its comparative analysis of Trump and Obama's inauguration speeches run by IBMer Jeremy Waite just hours after @POTUS45's was delivered was remarkable for many reasons – its speed, its length, and its counter-intuitive insights and conclusions. For all of those reasons, it was also remarkable for the tens of thousands of likes and shares it received. If you've not read it yet, put this book aside for the 40 minutes it'll take you to digest his blog. Search for "Waite Trump Obama", click on one of the many links, and enjoy.

Where language processing falls down and will doubtless continue to do so is in original content generation. Yes, it's true that algorithms have been written to scour news wire sources and compose articles for online publications; articles that human readers cannot detect as being written by non-humans. I know news journalists who are quaking in their shoes at this technology. But those algorithms and no algorithms yet conceived can come close to being brilliant organisational storytellers. The context, the nuance, the history, the purpose, the direction, the audience, the "news just in", all of these factors make me confident that crafting organisational stories in the language of humans will remain the preserve of people for the foreseeable future.

So, here are some examples of data-driven stories, from public and private sectors, that I truly believe read and sound human. As with the examples in Chapter 5, I've scored these on the Flesch–Kincaid reading ease scale too. I wanted to make the point one last time that simple, clear sentences with fewer, shorter words are so much more impactful.

Here's a great example of human chatter from the U.K. Home Office's Fire Kills campaign:[2]

> *Test your smoke alarms monthly. Last year over 200 people died in fires in the home. You're at least 4 times more likely to die in a fire in the home if there's no working smoke alarm. When you test your smoke alarms, you could test the smoke alarms of an older family member, neighbour or friend who needs help. It only takes a moment to test and gives your family and people you care about a better chance of surviving a fire.*
>
> (Flesch–Kincaid reading ease score 83.9 –
> see Chapter 1 for details)

Invoking discussion with neighbours and family members adds a human touch, allowing a serious – and highly important – message to be conveyed simply and effectively.

Cancer Research U.K. talks human in the next extract.[3] While maintaining a serious tone (as befits a cancer charity), this section has a conversational edge which feels friendly. It's easy to read and explains facts clearly.

> *We want survival in the UK to be among the best in the world. We're focusing our efforts in four key areas – working to help prevent cancer, diagnose it earlier, develop new treatments and optimise current treatments by personalising them and making them even more effective. We'll continue to support research into all types of cancer and across all age groups. And*

we're keeping our focus on understanding the biology of cancer so we can use this vital knowledge to save more lives.

(FK 54.3)

And finally, here are three, great examples of simple, clear, data-driven storytelling. The first one comes from those pioneers of brand storytelling, Innocent Drinks:[4]

We started innocent in 1999 after selling our smoothies at a music festival. We put up a big sign asking people if they thought we should give up our jobs to make smoothies, and put a bin saying "Yes" and a bin saying "No" in front of the stall. Then we got people to vote with their empties. At the end of the weekend, the "Yes" bin was full, so we resigned from our jobs the next day and got cracking. Since then we've started making coconut water, juice and kids' stuff, in our quest to make natural, delicious, healthy drinks that help people live well and die old.

(FK 77.6)

Second, from new kids on the home security block, Cocoon:[5]

Traditional home security doesn't work for most people. It's too expensive, too complicated, and false alarms happen so often that we've learnt simply to ignore them. In 2014, our founding team decided that the future of home security is to make using it as simple and intelligent as possible. We set about creating a technology that would protect the whole home from a single device, and this is how Cocoon came into the world. We believe in making homes safer and simpler. Often the people that need home security the most are the people that don't have access to it. Whether you're renting, own your home or travel between homes, everyone should feel safe at home with the minimum of fuss.

(FK 62.5)

And last of all, not sounding like a business at all, we have new wave cosmetics business, Lush.[6] The language combines a positive tone of voice with a straightforward line in storytelling. Focusing on the idea behind the brand makes it easy for the reader to forget they're being sold a product at all.

Here at Lush we have never liked to call ourselves an Ethical Company. We find the term rather a difficult concept, because it seems to us that it is used to describe companies who try not to damage people or planet with their trade practices – when surely this should not be regarded as "ethical" but as normal business-as-usual. All business should be ethical and all trade should be fair.

Individual companies should not stand out simply by not being damaging or unfair. No company should be trading from an unethical position and society has a right to expect as the norm fairness and resource stewardship from the companies that supply them. We always wish to conduct our business so that all people who have contact with us, from our ingredients suppliers through to our staff and customers, benefit from their contact with Lush and have their lives enriched by it. No company is perfect and we strive daily to get closer to the ideal vision that all Lush people share. We will always want and demand more from Lush, so that our business practices match our own expectations, our staff and customer expectations and the needs of the planet.

(FK 55.5)

SUMMING UP

Dan Pink is right. We're all in sales, whether we represent a business, a charity, or the public sector, whether we're a doctor looking to convince her patient to complete a course of medication or a teacher requiring students to complete homework tasks.

Organisations are abstract entities, but they're made up – primarily – of people. So, their language should be human, too.

But when they're put in the spotlight, many people produce words and content quite unlike normal human speech and communication.

Organisational storytellers often produce complex, difficult, confusing words for the following reasons: psychology, time pressure, projected norms, organisational structure, fear of getting it wrong, poor planning, jargon, and the language of statistics.

B2C businesses are generally good at talking clearly and simply to their customers, as well as to other external stakeholder groups. B2C talks human.

B2B businesses lag behind B2C in their ability and willingness to talk human. The justification (or excuse) is that they're talking about more complex, specialist issues. Not so.

TED talker Bryan Kramer says there is no B2B or B2C. It's now human-to-human or #H2H.

Use your storytelling to stimulate a response. Much better to get an outright rejection than a bland "Meh?" or a look of total incomprehension.

To tell a good story, you have to know your audience. Know how you should addresses them, what language you should use, and what your stories should be about.

Knowing your audience is all about empathy – the ability to put yourself in your audience's shoes using an organisational theory of mind.

Empathy is a – the – fundamental human quality, and corporate and brand storytellers should always have their empathy radar switched on.

Being empathetic in organisational storytelling is all about observing the principles of the Cocktail Party Rule.

The Cocktail Party Rule states that: "If you want to be boring, talk about yourself. If you want to be interesting, talk about what matters to those who are listening."

Think before you enter a room – before you open your mouth – before you put fingers to keyboard about who your audience is and what they want to get out of interacting with you. As well as what you want to get out of interacting with them.

Algorithms might be able to write the news. But they're very unlikely for the foreseeable future to take over an empathy-driven, data-driven, organisational storytelling role.

GIVE IT A GO: WHAT'S OUR "WHY?"

Have you ever considered what your organisation's real purpose is? I don't mean "to make money" or "to be the best". I mean its purpose. Its "Why?"

First, watch Simon Sinek's TEDx talk from Puget Sound 2009, "How great leaders inspire action".[7] Even if – like me – you've watched it dozens of times before, along with 35 million others. Next, get together a small and diverse team of different individuals in your organisation. Get them to watch it. And then go into a room with no phones or laptops or distractions of any sort and work out why it is your organisation exists.

Be ruthless and pressure-test the answer. If it's too bland or indistinctive, work at it some more. And when you've got something compelling and distinctive, get agreement from the organisation to get everyone in the enterprise to build on and share in and communicate your purpose. It will be truly transformative and the yardstick by which you judge future action.

DATA-DRIVEN STORIES

Campaign for Real Beauty

| **What's the organisation?** |
| Unilever |

| **What's the brand?** |
| Dove |

| **What's the campaign?** |
| Campaign for Real Beauty |

| **What's the story?** |
| Unilever's flagship beauty brand, Dove, was being beaten by its competitors. It needed to refresh its proposition and find a purpose. After several false starts, it chose to champion "real types not stereotypes" and tackle head-on the high-pressure tactics of the global beauty industry. |

| **How did data drive the story?** |
| The campaign was based on the research finding that, all around the world, only 2% of the world's women would describe themselves as beautiful. |

| **What was the outcome of the campaign?** |
| A brand rejuvenation. Purpose – to challenge the stereotypes of the beauty industry – built into the heart of new product development strategy. Millions of conversations with tweenage and teenage girls worldwide about beauty. The concept of purpose shifted to Unilever's corporate brand and many other product brands, too. CEO Paul Polman now leads a truly purpose-led organisation. |

So much has been written about Dove's Campaign for Real Beauty that – if this book didn't have the very clear purpose of demonstrating the power and impact of data-driven storytelling – it would be difficult to know where to start to write something new about it.

For years, Dove had been slowly losing market share to both non-branded competitors and, in its flagship market of North America in particular, to Nivea. Something had to be done to reverse the decline. In the early 2000s, lead advertising agency Ogilvy made a number of promising starts at looking to position Dove as the anti-beauty industry beauty industry brand champion. But the creative expression of the disruptive idea wasn't quite sticking.

Then Dove formed a strategic partnership with Joah Santos, the advertising creative reputed to have developed an approach to advertising known as "mission marketing". Santos led a multi-market research campaign working with leading academics around the world. From the wealth of data Dove generated from its research, the single most important nugget of data that provided the insight to create the Campaign for Real Beauty was this haunting statistic: in every market Dove asked the question, only 2% or fewer of all women described themselves as beautiful.

Dove set out on a mission to celebrate real beauty – the real, everyday beauty that lives inside every woman, and had a mantra to celebrate: "real types not stereotypes". This positioning set the brand in opposition to the overwhelming majority of the established beauty industry. From 2004 onwards, Dove launched wave after wave of films that tackled the issues of beauty industry, fashion industry, and fashion media attitudes to what defined beauty. The brands looked to help redefine beauty and women's attitudes to their own beauty, thereby enhancing their self-confidence.

The films Dove made – including *Evolution* (2006) and *Onslaught* (2008) and the most recent, *Real Beauty Sketches* (2013); you'll find them all on YouTube – hardly needed to be advertised. They contained such powerful messages that they quickly went viral. Billboard campaigns featuring non-traditional (for the beauty industry) images of women with tick boxes asked the public to consider whether they were: for an older woman "withered or wonderful?", for a redhead with freckles "flawed or flawless?", for another older woman with a mane of grey hair "grey or gorgeous?", and for two fuller-figured women "fat or fit?" and "extra-large or extra-sexy?" In the infancy and then early childhood of social media, people happily and spontaneously shared the billboards as well as the films, giving them vastly more exposure than had been paid for. Dove had started a movement.

The movement included the creation of an organisation called the Dove Self-Esteem Fund, which set out on its own mission – which it easily surpassed – to have millions of conversations with tweenage and teenage girls about what beauty meant to them and how they shouldn't be browbeaten into accepting stereotypical perceptions of beauty. All girls and women are beautiful, the campaign contended, still smarting from the original, killer statistic – still using that as the underpinning and justification for the campaign – and they should all celebrate that fact.

It took a little time for the campaign to translate into sales performance for Dove. When it really started to take off was when Unilever developed a new wave of products specifically designed for peri- and post-menopausal women, its Pro-Age range. From the very earliest days of the campaign, Dove had celebrated the beauty of older women. By creating a sub-brand tailored for this often-overlooked demographic and at the same time turning its name into a campaigning slogan ("At Dove we are Pro-Age"), the campaign was made to align with the product proposition. For there would have been no point in running a stunning, viral, socially responsible campaign that generated unprecedented levels of free publicity and yet didn't sell another tub of face cream.

The campaign was galvanic in recruitment and retention of staff within Unilever, and the challenge Dove faced was threefold: (a) no staff wanting to leave, (b) enormous numbers of staff wanting to transfer onto Dove from other Unilever brands, and (c) sack loads of unsolicited CVs and servers full of emails from marketers outside of Unilever wanting to join the cause. Real Beauty won all of the advertising world's top awards, including numerous Lions at Cannes. It was also named by U.S. trade publication *Ad Age* as one of the five best campaigns of the century.

Unilever's founding father, William Hesketh Lever, was the Victorian philanthropic businessman who built the model town of Port Sunlight on the Wirral for the workers at his Lever Brothers soap factories. Regular handwashing with soap was known in Victorian times to reduce sickness and even prevent death, even if the mechanism of bacterial infection was not properly understood. Lever was on a mission to make soap widely available to the masses, but like other Victorian businessmen in rapidly industrialising Britain – men like the Colmans of Norwich and the Cadburys and Bournevilles of Birmingham – he also believed successful businesses had both the opportunity and the responsibility to create sustainable and affordable housing for his workers near their places of work. Enlightened self-interest, of course. But real business on a mission or, as we've said time and again in this book, with a purpose.

Dove's conversion to mission marketing came at a pivotal time for Unilever. The company acquired Ben & Jerry's ice cream in 2000, a social enterprise from its foundation. After a couple of well-documented false starts, the company found meaningful roles for founders Cohen and his partner, Jerry Greenfield.

They brought mission-led marketing to all Unilever's brands and ultimately to its corporate brand. The success of Real Beauty and Unilever's conversion to purpose-led marketing enabled CEO Paul Polman to embed sustainability at the heart of the company's growth strategy. And it all started with the data-driven storytelling campaign, based on research about the world's women and real beauty.

Key takeaway: Sometimes what appears to be a small and insignificant nugget of insight can fuel a data-driven storytelling campaign so profound that it changes the direction of even the world's biggest businesses.

Note: After more than a decade of extraordinary, ground-breaking work, 2017 was something of an annus horribilis for Dove – at least in the U.K. – with three campaigns misfiring badly. The first used different body shapes as the basis to create actual bottles for products, the second gave a platform for critics of breastfeeding in public, and the third implied skin-lightening effects of a Dove body lotion. The brand needs to take care not to unpick the great work and good will engendered by the Campaign for Real Beauty.

NOTES

1 http://phrontistery.info/nonsense.html gives definitions to all these words in a glossary
2 https://firekills.campaign.gov.uk
3 http://bit.ly/2kIs8LF
4 http://bit.ly/1vx8bQo
5 https://cocoon.life
6 https://uk.lush.com/article/lush-ethical-company
7 http://bit.ly/1fJPwPe

7

FIVE GODS OF DATA-DRIVEN STORYTELLING

That's what we storytellers do. We restore order with imagination. We instil hope again and again and again.
Tom Hanks as Walt Disney in the 2013 movie *Saving Mr Banks*

ON THE IMPORTANCE OF BEING IMPORTANT

John Simmons is a significant figure in British corporate and brand storytelling. He founded the collective of business writers simply known as The Writer, as well as 26, a representative organisation for writers, editors, publishers, and language specialists. He's the author of notable books in the area of brand language and storytelling, including *Dark Angels*, *The Invisible Grail*, and *We, Me, Them, And It*. And he's a prolific trainer in the area of writing for business.

Many years ago, I was a delegate on one of John's writing courses. Now John believes in the "beautiful constraint"; that by putting boundaries and rules down on what you write and how you are allowed to express yourself, you can produce better, more interesting work. Among the many exercises John asked everyone on my course to perform, one has stuck with me for more than a decade. "Write a description of the god of your business!" John urged the financiers and pharmaceutical marketers and PR folk who filled the room. I probably wrote something about a quicksilver, Hermes-like figure, though as I was working in PR and had started there in the late 1980s, Dionysus might have been more appropriate.

John, of course, would be one of deities of the written word in business, along with Martin Clarkson of the Storytellers, and Peter Mandelson for his time revolutionising communications at the (new) Labour Party. There are others, too, I'm aware of, but, by and large, we're a difficult breed to track down and identify, preferring to be a hidden hand behind the businesses we write for. Like the archetype of Heracles – exemplified in James Bond, Han Solo, and Domestos – we do the dirty work to keep the real gods happy. And as for the verbal side of data-driven wordsmithery, I'd say the field is too early in its lifecycle for many to have more than demigod status.

But there are gods of data-driven storytelling who inspire our clan, gods who take data and make pictures with it that change the way we think about the subject areas they're focusing on, data more broadly, and the world in general. Their work has influenced governments and legislators, medical authorities and regulators, and individual members of the public to change their minds and take direct action. They are masters of the "moving business".

And while this book is not a how-to guide in data visualisation – and there are many, many of these, including some written by a couple of those singled out for god status in this chapter – it's important that we round out our discussion of data-driven storytelling by paying homage to those noble few who have done so much to tame and make better use of data through data visualisation. For just as lyrics are to music in songs, so pictures can be to words in narrative by numbers.

FLORENCE NIGHTINGALE

Ask most people who have been educated in the U.K. what they know about Florence Nightingale, and they'll tell you that she was a very important figure in nursing. During the Crimean War, she pioneered advances in nursing in the theatre of war that lived through Vietnam and on to even contemporary theatres of conflict. They might know that her work also changed practice in regular hospitals, too. And the slightly older ones will tell you she used to be on the back of the old £10 note, celebrating her extraordinary work during the Crimean War.

What they're very unlikely to be able to tell you is that she was also a pioneer of data-driven storytelling. Having put in place a wide range of very practical measures to reduce the spread of infection and disease in British military field hospitals – from improving ventilation to removing rotting animal carcases that had been blocking the water supply – Nightingale observed and recorded the fact that mortality rates of the injured dropped dramatically in response to her interventions. Dedicated to understanding cause and effect, she kept meticulous records of the deaths from wounds, diseases, and other causes among the soldiers under her care.

Keen to share her findings with the military authorities and even Queen Victoria herself, Nightingale realised she needed to develop a new and visual way to present her findings that wouldn't have non-specialist, non-statisticians glazing over with boredom. She was on a mission to change field hospital policy across the army in order to give otherwise healthy, fit, and strong men the best possible chance of survival

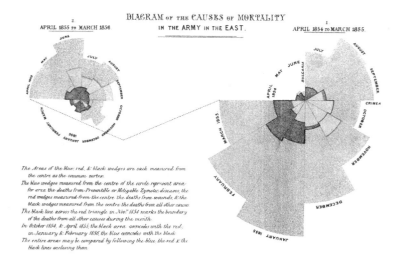

Figure 7.1 Florence Nightingale

Florence Nightingale's pioneering coxcomb design that changed hospital design

after injury. She couldn't bear the fact that many – without her types of intervention – died needlessly through lack of sanitation and poor field hospital design.

So rather than present her findings in tedious tables of data or standard bar charts, she devised novel ways of representing and visualising the data that enabled her to tell her story at a glance. Julie Rehmeyer explains[1] Nightingale's revolutionary coxcomb visualisation in a 2008 edition of *Science News:*

> *Each month is represented as a twelfth of a circle. Months with more deaths are shown with longer wedges, so that the area of each wedge represents the number of deaths in that month from wounds, disease or other causes. For months during the first part of the war, the blue wedges, representing disease, are far larger than either the red ones (for wounds) or the black ones (for other causes). For months after March 1855, when the Sanitary Commission arrived, the blue wedges start becoming dramatically smaller.*

Nightingale said her coxcomb graph was designed "to affect through the eyes what we fail to convey to the public through their word-proof ears". While I'd never accept that it's impossible to use words and words alone to build and make a convincing, data-driven argument, sometimes a killer chart works alongside a killer statistic or analysis. Nightingale's data visualisation was certainly impactful. Her coxcomb led to fundamental changes in how both field hospitals and fixed, domestic hospitals are designed and operate. All through a little bit of effective, data-driven storytelling, sprinkled with the emotion of saving young men's lives.

DR JOHN SNOW

Our second deity is another Victorian, this time the physician Dr John Snow, one of the founding members of the Epidemiological Society of London.

In the middle of the nineteenth century, there was a devastating cholera outbreak in Soho. Hard though it is to imagine today, the provision of mains water plumbing and clean and safe water was still under development and roll-out. Even 175 years ago, the Industrial Revolution was still to have its effect, even in significant parts of central London. People had to collect their water from water pumps.

By talking to locals, Snow identified that the origin of this particular outbreak and spread of the disease was a water pump on Broad Street, and he convinced the authorities to disable the water pump by removing its handle. Because the germ theory of disease had not yet been discovered, Snow was unaware of the mechanism of transmission of cholera from the water pump. But by visualising the number of deaths occurring in the vicinity of the water pump with his now legendary dot map, he was able to demonstrate the source of the infection and the spread of disease. The map, reproduced below, shows one dot per death by cholera,

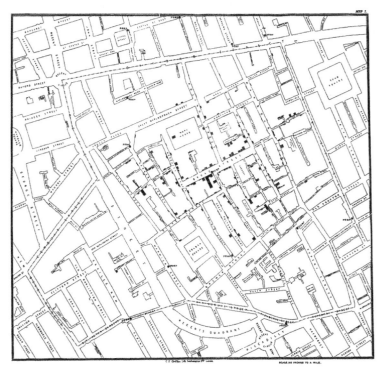

Figure 7.2 John Snow
Dr John Snow's dot map of cholera outbreaks related to a tainted water pump in Soho, 1854

with the intensity of dots increasing with greater proximity to the infected water pump. Snow was able to prove that the water company was bringing water taken from parts of the River Thames polluted with sewerage and distributing it to the water pump in Broad Street.

Snow used a compelling visualisation of data he collected – after being tipped off by local residents about the source of their drinking water – to tell a powerful, evidence-based, policy-changing story. What's more, his work led to the establishment of one of the most important and impactful branches of medicine: epidemiology.

HANS ROSLING

God number three is another epidemiologist, the impish, infectiously enthusiastic, and sadly recently deceased Hans Rosling.

Rosling learned about disease, poverty, the impact of family size on life prospects, and much more besides by working as a researcher and medical officer in some of the most challenging and under-served parts of the developing world, including India, Mozambique, and the Democratic Republic of the Congo. He spent more than 20 years studying and characterising the epidemiology of konzo, a paralytic disease that leads to permanent disability of the limbs, particularly the legs.

He came to international prominence thanks to his mission to make sense of complex global heath data sets through dynamic, animated visualisations. His approach was to present, clearly and straightforwardly, multiple variables interacting simultaneously, such as time, wealth, disease, geography, and life-expectancy.

Rosling and his children founded the Gapminder Foundation, an NGO that promotes sustainable development through better understanding of statistics about social, economic, and environmental development. Gapminder – named in honour of the London Underground safety announcement, "Mind the gap" – is also the open-access repository of vast public health data sets. They are made available to encourage researchers – indeed, anyone with an interest or an idea – around the world to use the data to make sense of the world and put forward possible solutions.

Gapminder also developed pioneering Trendalyzer software platform using Rosling's trademark bubble and motion charts that help make so

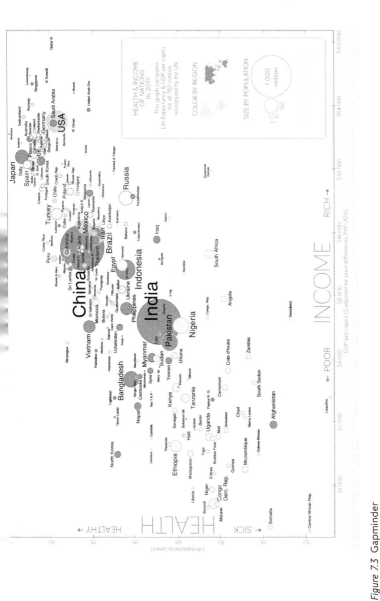

Figure 7.3 Gapminder

Mind the gap: output from Hans Rosling's Trendalyzer software, showing time (year), life expectancy (Y-axis), every country in the world (dots), region (colour), population (relative size of bubble), and GDP per capita (X-axis). African countries are in dark blue (lowest life expectancy and GDP).

much sense out of multivariate data sets. Although acquired by Google in 2007, elements of Trendalyzer are available for public use. A typical output is shown above.

Rosling's public lectures were delivered with a trademark blend of humour, extreme clarity, and an infectious sense that because he understood the world so clearly, so could you. His TED Talks and BBC documentary, *The Joy of Stats*, have all been watched millions of times, and mostly by those who are neither epidemiologists or statisticians. If you've not seen them, get over to YouTube now.

EDWARD TUFTE

Edward Tufte is Professor Emeritus of Political Science, Statistics, and Computer Science at Yale. He's been described as "the Leonardo da Vinci of data" by the *New York Times* and – not to be outdone – "the Galileo of graphics" by *Business Week*.

I first came across Tufte when a friend and mentor gave me a copy of his wonderful book – big, square, LP-sized, more of a manifesto – *The Cognitive Style of PowerPoint*. It's a treatise against the ubiquity of PowerPoint based on the way that the strictures and templates of PowerPoint make us think dumber. "Slideware," Tufte says, "reduces the analytical quality of presentations . . . weakens spatial and visual reasoning, and almost always corrupts statistical analysis."

Tufte is the closest the world has to a philosopher – perhaps a philosopher king – of data visualisation. But that doesn't make him a recherché recluse with no understanding of the dynamics of pragmatics of business. Far from it. He's a philosopher of the stripe of Alain de Botton, concerned that his thinking about thinking can shake the frustrated mainstream out of their torpor of data presentation hell and into the sunny uplands of mutual understanding. That makes him a man committed to showing mere mortals how to use, share, and understand information better. To have shorter, more meaningful, more impactful meetings and, in that way, achieve more.

Tufte's workshops promise a lot, including "fundamental design strategies for all information displays: sentences, tables, diagrams, maps, charts,

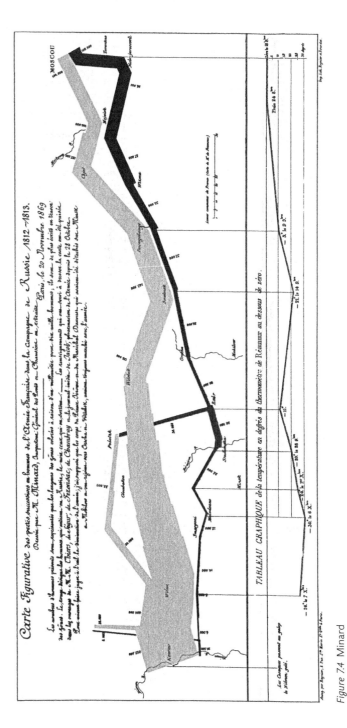

Figure 7.4 Minard

Minard's map of Napoleon's 1812 Russian campaign – an early but exceptional data visualisation

images, video, data visualizations, and randomized displays for making graphical statistical inferences." What's more, Tufte believes that – done right – data visualisations communicate what prose alone cannot.

Tufte uses a broad array of visualisations, including maps, graphs, charts, and tables like Minard's map of Napoleon's failed Russian campaign of 1812, shown in Figure 7.4. The line radiating from the Western front to Moscow and back again conveys the following variables: time, trajectory, size of the army (thickness of the bar; as it gets thinner, French soldiers are dying from Russian attack, famine, and the cold), temperature over time, and even two splinter campaigns. Advance for the main bulk of the army and the two splinter campaigns is shown in grey; retreat is shown in black.

For Tufte, data visualisation and presentation are very much about the giver and the receiver, and about the empathy required for the former to enable the latter to understand, be moved, and get benefit from what the former shares. It's very much a two-way street, and he provides strategies for spectatorship and consuming reports and data every bit as much as he gives advice about how to share and present data to an audience.

All his books are recommended reading, starting with the classic *The Visual Display of Quantitative Information*.

DAVID McCANDLESS

At the end of a warm day in May 2014, I queued up outside the splendid Georgian folly that is Brighton Pavilion, clutching the ticket that would admit me to the 1,700-seater Dome theatre. Over 20 years in Sussex, I've seen this capacious auditorium host everyone from the Bootleg Beatles to Marc Ronson, the London Philharmonic to a couple of TEDx curate's eggs.

But that spring evening, there was an extra crackle in the air. The others in the queue were more fanlike than any audience I'd experienced at the Dome before. Plus, there were more piercings and many more beards – long, expertly sculpted, like French footballer Olivier Giroud's or Zeus', only much, much bigger – than I'd seen ever in one place. It was as if all of Brighton's digerati had left their desks and studios in Silicon Seaside and flocked to see their all-time favourite act. None other than the unassuming rock god of data-driven storytelling, David McCandless. This Arts Desk review[2] of the event captures it well.

McCandless is the author of the peerless *Information Is Beautiful*, followed up since he rocked Brighton by *Knowledge Is Beautiful*. He's created and run and sold several different businesses in the data-driven storytelling area, and his current passion is VIZsweet ("visualisation suite" – geddit?), which describes itself as "a high-end cloud-based tool for creating beautiful, interactive data-visualizations".

His purpose is to use data visualisation and information design to tell stories. Before running his own businesses, he was a data journalist for both *Wired* and the *Guardian*, where he was one of the core team behind the newspaper's Data Lab, a power-player in data visualisation and data-driven storytelling in the first half of the twenty-teens. Sadly, cuts by the *Guardian*'s owners, the Scott Trust – which loses tens of millions a year on the title – have put paid to the Data Lab.

In Chapter 2, we considered the fact that when numbers get too big, they lose their meaning (a phenomenon that McCandless' visualisations deal with routinely). Talking about the totality of U.K. Government spending, I concluded that £750bn was "a number so far outside most people's grasp or comprehension that it just becomes a circular definition." In May 2010, the *Guardian* Data Lab produced a stunning visualisation of U.K. public spending 2008–9, which I strongly recommend you go and seek out and download.[3] The visualisation was published before then-Chancellor Gideon Osbourne had made the promised cuts to public spending as part of the Coalition Government's so-called austerity so-called strategy. The visualisation was intended to inform the *Guardian*'s readers exactly where U.K. plc was spending at the time and what the cuts might mean for their priority areas.

Even though the figure was at the time almost a fifth smaller than it is today, it still clocked in at a mind-bending £620.7bn. And although McCandless' visualisation doesn't make it simple to understand, it does give a very helpful sense of scale and priorities for Government, with the top five spenders:

1   Department of Work and Pensions, £135.7bn
2   HM Treasury, £109.5bn

3   Department of Health, £109.4bn
4   Department for Children, Schools & Families, £63.18bn
5   Ministry of Defence, £44.6bn

What's more, the infographic was printed on the double-page, centre spread of the Berliner-sized paper. As well as making an attractive poster, its life-sized version easily enabled closer scrutiny when stuck to the wall. You could get the big picture from the overall illustration, and then drill down on particular departments you were interested in.

The visualisation is echt McCandless who, despite his rock-star status, remains humble and accessible – in person at his talks, and via his presence on Reddit, here http://bit.ly/2ov5K8w.

SUMMING UP

The words attributed by the makers of the movie *Saving Mr Banks* to Walt Disney summarise precisely what the best data-driven storytellers achieve with their visualisations: "instilling hope again and again and again".

For a godless man like me, data-driven storytelling deities come in different forms, from different places, and from different eras. Technology is relevant, but not necessary, and it can often prove to be a distraction. Florence Nightingale, John Snow, and Edward Tufte's favourite, Minard, drew everything by hand, but that doesn't make their data-driven storytelling any less accurate, impactful, or clear. Yes, technology allows you to do more in a shorter time, both in terms of data analysis and visualisation. Big Data tools and technologies take the drudgery of data analysis, improve the speed exponentially from slow human hands and eyes to gigaflops of processing speed. They also remove the opportunity for human error.

But when you're looking to tell stories with data and statistics, technology should never be your starting point. As discussed in Chapter 3, data-driven storytelling is never, initially, a technology problem. It's a problem of purpose, a challenge to identify and articulate your purpose in the data-driven story you're looking to tell. Finding your inner "Why?"

If you know why you want to make a particular case – if you know whom you want to move to do what – you'll soon discover what you want to say. How you're going to say it – what data sets, which statistical test, what analytics tools, which data visualisation platforms and packages you use – all that will fall into place. The more often you do it, the more quickly you'll discover your favourites. And remember Steve Jobs' founding purpose for Apple that we touched on in Chapter 3: "to remove the barrier of having to learn to use a computer". Keep that in mind, and make technology your slave, not your master – which just happens to be another of Apple's declared purposes over time.

Then you come to your other, and perhaps the most important, "how". What's the story going to be like? Is it a three-act structure, a hero's journey? What role do data and statistics play in supporting your core narrative? What's the killer statistic and the money-shot chart? How do you resist the temptation of throwing more and more facts – more and more data – at the audience? How do you talk as a human, about human issues, in human language? What role does emotion play (probably a much bigger one that you ever imagined)? And is your empathy radar turned up to 11 to make sure you're thinking every bit as much as a receiver as you are a transmitter of information.

If you take this approach to data-driven storytelling, I'll warrant you'll become a master of the "moving business", persuading more people to see the world from your point of view. Standing on the shoulder of the giants we've met briefly in this chapter, you might just attain demi-god status within your own organisation. It's got to be worth a shot.

NOTES

1 http://bit.ly/1ldD73v
2 http://bit.ly/2pcwgBT
3 http://bit.ly/2oYyYee

8

WHY FACTS MATTER MORE THAN EVER

Either write something worth reading or do something worth writing about.
Benjamin Franklin, *Washington DC Evening Star*,
7 January 1853

The 2016 victories of both Vote Leave and Donald Trump were unexpected, to say the least. They were, in Benjamin Franklin's words, most definitely worth writing about, even if the media – and particularly the social media – content produced by both campaigns are less likely to stand the test of time.

Brexit–Trump were behind in the opinion polls in the weeks leading up to both votes – sometimes a long way behind.

The polling industry, political pundits, most of the media, and most strikingly of all the bookmakers were predicting Remain–Hillary, not Brexit–Trump. Even after Brexit, and even after Trump declared just ahead of polling day that the 2016 Presidential election would be "Brexit Plus Plus Plus". It was.

Sure, the polls tightened as the election got closer. The polls always do that. Pollsters get more nervous as their reputations get put to the test.

Well, in these two elections, the pollsters almost all got it spectacularly wrong. Even Nate Silver – right in 49 out of 50 congressional districts in 2008 and all 50 in 2012 – didn't call for Trump. Admittedly, he and his 538 crew were among the least wrong. But in the polling business, being "least wrong" is a bit like being "half pregnant". Or buying a chocolate teapot.

Brexit–Trump has caused an existential crisis in the polling industry, indeed in much of the research business where political punditry has its home. The smart folks that help brands know which ads are likely to work best, what consumers want out of their next car, and which trends will shape the next season/year/decade are all scrabbling around to reinvent themselves and their methodologies. Much of that scrabbling feels like moving the deckchairs on the *Titanic*.

Yet I sense that some of this panic may be excessive, if understandable. Organisations will continue to need research and understanding and insight. They just might need a few more reassurances from their vendors – and they might treat them a little meaner than they have historically – until confidence is restored.

But there's no denying that Brexit–Trump was seismic, and the aftershocks will continue to reverberate around the world long after no one can remember who Nigel Farage was. And they'll also echo way beyond the polling and market research industry.

POST-TRUTH, FAKE NEWS

One of the defining aspects of Brexit–Trump was the fall and fall of facts and the growing lack of importance placed by candidates on evidence and data and, well, the truth. As we observed in Chapter 2, Michael Gove contended during the EU Referendum campaign that "people in this country have had enough of experts". Facts, we were told, did not matter. They mattered so little that, when the Vote Leave campaign chose to use their own – like the purported £350m weekly contribution from U.K. plc to EU Inc. which the Leavers pledged to redirect to fund the NHS – they turned out to be not so much truths as untruths. Gross, not net figures. Or – to be candid – lies.

Time and again during Trump on the stump, when facts were used, they turned out to be as reliable as those pedalled by the Brexiteers.

Ever since, forensic examination of the supporters and consultants and technologies underpinning both campaigns – and supporting the dissemination of these true lies – have been found to be the same businesses. Conspiracy theories rage all around.

As a result, ever since Brexit–Trump, there's been a concern – in much of the media, not just the liberal wing; in academia; in the polling industry; and in the broad research community – that, if elections can be won by either no facts or lies, we must have entered a post-truth society. It didn't seem like the world was heading in this direction, and then all of a sudden, the rules of engagement have been turned upside down and what applied before doesn't apply any more. Whereas people tuned into the BBC and CNN to get their news in previous elections, apparently they're now happy to get their fake news regurgitated via Facebook and Google. Has the world gone dumb?

The well-established oracle of the twenty-teens Wikipedia describes "**Post-truth politics** (also called **post-factual politics**)" as "a political culture in which debate is largely framed by appeals to emotion disconnected from details of policy, and the repeated assertion of talking points to which factual rebuttals are ignored". As we've already observed, "post-truth" was the Oxford English Dictionary's "word" of the year for 2016.

As someone setting out his stall as a data-driven storyteller, you might think I'd be worried. Throughout this book, I've talked repeatedly about the importance of using data and statistics to form the foundations and underpinning for organisational storytelling. Surely (you might be tempted to argue) if people don't want and don't care for facts in elections – which, in theory, determine the shape, colour, and direction of their country of residence for at least the next four years – they won't give a fig for the facts any organisation might care to share with them.

In fact, I couldn't disagree more strongly. We live at a time when facts have never mattered more. But as I've said time and again throughout this book, arguments are not won by facts and facts alone. On our journey, we talked a little about rhetoric and the skills of the orator. In fourth century BC Athens and first century BC Rome, Demosthenes and Cicero were the leading figures in the "moving business"; professional orators, politicians, and their societies' leading legal eagles.

Facts mattered very much to the cases that they were making, but form mattered just as much as content. As anyone who's ever read (a translation of) *The Philippics* or *Against Cataline* will know, it's not one damn fact after another that sways and wins the day. There's a huge amount of emotion involved, too. And it's these twin barrels of rationality and emotionality that hold the key to the most effective form of storytelling. For politicians and for organisations of all stripes.

David McCandless, one of our five gods of data visualisation, learned some of his trade while at the *Guardian*'s late, lamented Data Blog. That blog carried the strapline "Facts are sacred". In that, they were right. Just as Sense About Science is right in its mission to promote respect for scientific evidence and good science. But as the *New Scientist* observed in its hair-shirted editorial in the immediate aftermath of Brexit, "For reason to triumph, scientists need to learn to engage with emotion". Cognitive psychology shows us that the more we try to convince people that we're right and they're wrong with fact after fact after fact, the more they'll dig in their heels and look for evidence that reinforces their own position to enable them to reject ours.

The heady mixture of fact and emotion – evidence-based persuasion – is what was behind April 2017's March for Science (https://satellites. marchforscience.com). In the first three months of the Trump presidency, @POTUS45: started to dismantle Obama's Clean Power Plan; abolished a rule requiring large federal agencies to consider how large federal projects affect climate change; made swingeing cuts to the Environmental Protection Agency (among other bodies) from an annual "$8.1bn to $5.7bn, eliminating a quarter of the agency's 15,000 jobs";[1] failed to appoint a special scientific adviser; and appointed to head of the EPA one Scott Pruitt, who had stated publicly before his appointment that he doesn't accept that CO_2 emissions are a primary cause of climate change. Throughout his presidential campaign, Trump repeatedly called climate change a hoax.

Three months into the new administration, the U.S. (and global) scientific community had had enough. There were hundreds of rallies around the world under the banner of the March for Science. When scientists take to the streets in an out-of-character, emotional outpouring, data-driven storytellers can reflect that the community most closely associated with evidence-based narrative have got the message. President of the Union of Concerned Scientists, Kenneth Kimmell, wrote in the *Observer* that the March for Science represented a significant fightback against Trump's "unprecedented attack on science, scientists and evidence-based policy making [that is] underway in the U.S. federal Government".[2] The worm has turned, and it's learned – unlike the Remain campaigners – to present rationality with a veneer or sugar-coating of emotionality.

The reasoned yet emotional, academic fightback against fake news is captured nowhere better than in a new course at the University of Washington entitled *Calling Bullshit In the Age of Big Data* (see http://callingbullshit.org). The course is run across two schools by Carl T. Bergstrom and Jervin West from the Information School and the Department of Biology. The course aims to redress the balance in academia and public life where – as they say, "politicians are unconstrained by facts and science is conducted by press release (not journals)".

This new course – which operates as a MOOC and so is available to any citizen of the world with a Wi-Fi connection – is designed to equip the next generation of graduates with the critical faculties they need to call bullshit on the misuse of data and statistics in public discourse. It should be compulsory viewing for every student of anything everywhere.

In the first lecture of the course – and they're all available on YouTube – Bergstrom and Jervin use a 1710 quote from the satirist and essayist Jonathan Swift to discuss the Pizzagate debacle from the 2016 presidential elections: "Falsehood flies, and the Truth comes limping after it". Fake news (falsehoods) travel faster than truths.

To refresh your memories on Pizzagate: Comet Ping Pong, a pizzeria in Washington D.C., was said to be harbouring a paedophile ring with connections to Hillary Clinton. The accusations led a "concerned citizen" to run into the restaurant and start shooting. Even though no one was injured, that's hardly the point. And even though this bizarre conspiracy theory has been completely refuted and rejected – including by those who were helping to spread it – concerned U.S. citizens repeatedly turn up at the White House wearing t-shirts showing they believe that Pizzagate is true and they want to take action against it.

To repeat Swift's maxim: "Falsehood flies, and the Truth comes limping after it". Bergstrom and Jervin are to be applauded for using deliberately emotional language (and content) to stimulate interest and take up in their data-driven storytelling course. They also make a very good point about the permanence of stories and images online, and that the stench of fake news lingers longer than idle gossip did in a pre-mediated, pre-digital age.

FIGHTING BACK AGAINST FAKE NEWS

The battle against fake news is not insignificant, and it's my hope (not a strategy, I know) that *Narrative by Numbers* can do a little bit to help in this battle. Producing evidence-based narrative in a veneer of emotional wrapping is my prescription for using the twin skills of analytics plus storytelling to have lasting influence. But I'm not arrogant enough to think I'll succeed alone.

The mainstream media – until Trump's constant sneering and sniping, the trusted brands and touchstones of truth – have a significant role to play in countering fake news. To be clear, Trump has rather a narrow definition of fake news. He tends to mean any reporting that is of others' agendas and not his own, reporting that paints his idiosyncratic decision-making and approach to governance in anything other than a glowing light (i.e. not the alt.right). And while Trump is the trumpet voluntary of fake news, he and his supporters are not the only players in the game. It's just that – as the journalist Christiane Amanpour said[3] in a recent interview with TED's Chris Anderson – when the single most powerful individual in the free world cuts so fast and loose with the truth, that legitimises other less reputable leaders to adopt similar or lower standards. Her nightmare vision is of a race to the bottom. I'm not so pessimistic.

Separately, the apparent creation of hundreds of bogus social media profiles by Russian agents – with the express purpose of promulgating and sharing fake news in order to highjack the legitimate functioning of Western democracies – needs addressing by the social platforms themselves. Post Trump's election, some governments – most notably

Emmanuel Macron's in France – have taken a stand and been vigilant enough to root out some elements of the fake news underbelly.

For many years, Facebook, Twitter, and Google – including Google-owned YouTube – have deliberately described themselves as channels and means of distribution, rather than publishers. That protest is starting to wear thin when both independent and external investigations have revealed the extent of Russian and alt.right influence in using their platforms to share fake news. This argument is wearing particularly thin, given that these same platforms have clearly been shown to benefit financially from the ads served on fake news sites and profiles they carry and enable.

But the media worm is also starting to turn in the battle against fake news, and the establishment news outlets have a significant role to play in countering it. They can do this by re-establishing their status as touchstones of free and independent thinking, devoid of politicking and partisanship. However Trump may sneer in news conferences at the BBC, the *New York Times*, CNN, and the *Guardian*, these institutions have a role and a responsibility to point out what is fake and what is not, and they're rising to this challenge and in so doing re-establishing their role in both news and in truth vs lies.

For instance, the speed with which bogus reports about the Vegas mass murderer Stephen Paddock were debunked – reports in corners of the alt.right dark web that said Paddock was a Democrat and making an anti-Trump statement by shooting more than 500 people at a country music festival – was dizzying. And deeply encouraging. It took less than 12 hours for the first reporting against the fake news to appear, and after 24 hours, most of the offending – and wrong – content was no longer online.

THE ROLE OF ESTABLISHED NEWS BRANDS – OLD, AND NEW

And more than just rapid rebuttal, news organisations are becoming part of the anti-fake news machinery. One very good and very strong example is the permanent Reality Check team established by then head of BBC News, James Harding, in January 2017. The purpose of the dozens-strong unit is to fact-check and debunk deliberately misleading content that masquerades as news.

Harding said at the time of launch:

> *The BBC can't edit the internet, but we won't stand aside either. We will fact check the most popular outliers on Facebook, Instagram and other social media . . . Where we see deliberately misleading stories masquerading as news, we'll publish a Reality Check that says so. And we want Reality Check to be more than a public service, we want it to be hugely popular. We will aim to use styles and formats – online, on TV and on radio – that ensure the facts are more fascinating and grabby than the falsehoods.*

Facebook and other platforms that have been used to share fake news are also starting to take their responsibilities seriously. This is in part seen in the internal investigations they are running to assess how they were hacked by Russia in the 2016 presidential election. But it is also seen in the initiatives they are taking to help its users spot and understand what is fake and what is genuine, and to report and act against clearly fake content. Time will tell whether this self-regulatory approach is strong enough to deal with the fake news phenomenon. The only shame is that it took Facebook so long to take part (and so – even tangentially – admit its role), and that they insist on their own definition of the problem as "false news".

WHAT THIS ALL MEANS FOR NARRATIVE BY NUMBERS

More generally, though, the communications business appears to have been ahead of even technology platforms and the scientific community. From the *Mad Men* era of David Ogilvy and Bill Bernbach onwards, it's long been known that for campaigns to succeed they need to balance and blend the rational and the emotional. For Remain–Hillary, perhaps, the world view was just far too rational, while the opposition to these rational arguments was emotion all the way.

For Brexit–Trump, the orchestrators revved emotion to the max, as emotion (excuse me) trumped rationality. Yes, Brexit–Trump used facts, even if they were, ultimately, lies. But Brexit–Trump's empathy radar was more finely attuned to their electorates than Remain–Hillary's, which was mind-blind by comparison. They thought more about their audience and their opponents' audience and most particularly the audience of floating voters in the middle for whom emotions overpowered evidence.

The world has changed and lurched to the right, but facts and data and statistics and analytics haven't suddenly become redundant, just as voters haven't suddenly become idiots.

The need for everyone in the "moving business" to understand this and learn how to more finely calibrate emotion and facts is upon us.

And provided our empathy radar is on and we're thinking about everyone we're communicating with, then, do you know what, I'm pretty sure everything's going to be alright.

"Once upon a time there was a bold and courageous statistician . . ."

NOTES

1 http://nyti.ms/2onrPpA
2 http://bit.ly/2oziw4e
3 www.ted.com/talks/christiane_amanpour_how_to_seek_truth_in_the_era_of_
   fake_news

EPILOGUE

On a fresh but grey afternoon in early March 2017, I was sitting for the first time in the Meeting House of the University of Sussex. This was surprising for three reasons.

Surprise number one – This was the first time I'd set foot in this stunning building, and, dull as the day was outside, it was alive with light dancing through a rainbow of single-colour stained glass windows. At that moment, I'd lived in Sussex for nearly 20 years. What's more, I spent most of the first four years of the early Noughties studying and researching at the University, first for a master's and then for a doctorate in Experimental Psychology.

During my studies, day after day – as I used more and more data to tell better and better stories about the effects of alcohol and memory – I'd walk or ride or scuttle past this intriguing, circular building. But I never went in, curious at its architecture but put off by its religious associations. Architecture can do that to a godless man. My revelation at the building's beauty on my first visit made me curse my narrowmindedness. I should have remembered that the gods tend to get the best buildings, from the Parthenon to Pantheon, Stonehenge to L'Église Saint-Eustache.

Surprise number two – The man whose life we were celebrating in the Meeting House had a philosophy of education that, for the

Figure 9.1 Meeting House

first time, made sense of the multiple paths I've pursued in my own schooling, my work, and my life. Asa Briggs, Lord Briggs of Lewes, left Oxford in the late 1950s to set up "Oxford by the sea", or so family legend claims he called out as he headed south with a spade and unbounded optimism. Soon he was Vice Chancellor of the new university.

Because I'd come to Sussex with one aim in mind – to add scientific rigour and understanding to a mind that had taken a different path at school and university; I was a Classicist first time around – I had chosen Sussex for reasons about me, not reasons about the institution.

Retraining after a decade in the workplace following graduation, I had determined with the help of an excellent organisation called Career Psychology to pursue, erm, a career in psychology. Perhaps sometimes I can be a bit literal. I chose Sussex because it had one of the best three master's courses in psychology in the country, because they offered me a place after I taught myself the first-year course and sat an exam, and because it was four miles up the road from new centre of our universe in Lewes. I chose Sussex for a combination of academic and practical reasons, not because what it espoused as an educational philosophy: the mantra (for want of a better word) of interdisciplinarity.

When Briggs was given the task of creating the academic infrastructure of Sussex, he coined the phrase "redrawing the map of learning". One of the crucial elements of his approach was to ensure that students of any subject didn't just study narrowly in that one subject area. As in the best of North American universities, students would major in one area and minor in another. Briggs was passionate about what thinking about one subject could do in helping to draw connections and make breakthroughs in others. He was, among other things, the Professor of Mash-up, and his long shadow ensures this principle lives loud at the University today, 55 years after foundation.

I didn't know that when I chose Sussex. I wanted an environment in which I could move from my narrow classical background and become psychological. Nor did I know that while I was studying and researching there. But during Briggs' memorial service in the Meeting House, the theme came up time and time again. Colleagues, students, collaborators – all sang his praises as the champion of interdisciplinarity. Of the man who made them see the value of considering problems of social history through the lens of poetry, mathematics via apiculture, French literature via genetics.

An unhelpful recruitment consultant once described my CV as chaotic, labelling me "unplaceable". This was the mid-1990s, when moving from a PR firm to a trade association made small-minded recruiters find it hard to understand such giant leaps. It was as if – in Steven Berkoff's memorable description of poorly applied make-up – my CV had been typed by "a drunken epileptic on a rollercoaster".

When I heard the praise for Briggs in the Sussex Meeting House that dull spring day, my own choices to blend classics with hardcore biology and statistics made perfect sense. I understood why I'd done it. And I understood perfectly what I could do with it, and share with others. All the tools and techniques I'd picked up along the way – from reading Aristotle to analysis of variance, from Tacitus to t-tests – are ways of making sense of the world, of using evidence to tell stories. They're all just languages and codes for cleverer, clearer communication with real impact and emotion.

I was drawn to Briggs' memorial service for a number of reasons. He'd known my father at Oxford in the 1950s. After a first degree in Mods & Greats (Latin and Greek to anyone outside of Oxford) in the 1930s, my father returned to that university in the late 1940s to set up and run the Institute of Economics and Statistics. Of course he did. The natural next step for a curious Renaissance man like Kenneth Knowles, who also saw both beauty and story structure in numbers.

When I was starting secondary school, my father was retired from Oxford, spending his time engraving church windows and inventing Gothic typefaces. Whenever I stumbled across a subject I couldn't quite understand and I'd exhausted the extensive library at home, I'd ask my father what I should do. Remember, this was many years before the domestic internet.

"Call Geoffrey!" my father would say, writing his number of a scrap of paper. Geoffrey was a friend who knew something about the subject – perhaps slavery in Sparta – and he could help me out. I'd call Geoffrey and introduce myself as my father's son, and without exception, I'd be welcomed into a conversation of what felt like peers. I'd scribble notes and crack the question and thank Geoffrey and put the phone down. Then I'd report back to my father that Geoffrey had, indeed, been very helpful. And as I turned to go and write my essay on slavery in Sparta, I'd ask my father, "And who is Geoffrey?" He'd look up from his crossword and reply, "Oh, I think he's now the Emeritus Professor of Greek History at Oxford. Geoffrey de Ste Croix."

I quickly came to learn not to ask the job title of those my father suggested I call before I called them. And I remember very clearly the industrial revolution quandary I was in when my father said, "Call Asa!" and gave me a number that began with a Sussex prefix.

When we moved to Sussex, to Lewes, ten years after my father died, I was impressed by an imposing house at the foot of a steep hill and at the bottom of our road. I was even more impressed by the collection of Maoist statues in the window. And it didn't take more than four or five years before I found out that the inhabitant was one Lord Briggs of Lewes. What serendipity! We corresponded warmly, and though we never met, I felt secure and happy in the knowledge that he lived at the end of my road. Every time I passed it, I heard my long-dead father's encouragement to "Call Asa!"

So, I was drawn to the memorial service by family and personal connections, by my time at Sussex, by respect. I didn't know more than a handful of faces in the crowd, but it felt good and right to be there. And I was delighted to have this breakthrough insight during the service that gave meaning to my educational and career choices, all channelled through Asa. Storytelling plus data analysis equals data-driven storytelling. It's a classic example of interdisciplinarity in microcosm.

> **Surprise number three** – It is possible for a godless man to have a quasi-religious experience in a church. As the light came through the windows of the meeting house, I was like "Joliet" Jake Blues in *The Blues Brothers* when he understands why they simply have to put the band back together.

For much of my career, I've been drawn to and involved in storytelling. I've always read and looked for patterns and learnings from experience. And I've always written. I've written a lot. The diversion back to university, retraining as an experimental psychologist, gave me the ability to look at a set of numbers – including table after table of Big Data spreadsheets – and then do the "Where's Wally?" bit and find the nuggets of insight that unlock the story. To mine data sets to find the evidence base to tell a more convincing, more compelling, evidence-based story. One that moves people to do something in response because it's grounded in truth born of facts.

As I trust I've shown throughout this book, I truly do believe that these skills are among the most important for business today, and will prove to be even more critical in the years ahead. My personal journey may have been chaotic and unpredictable – at least for conservative recruitment consultants of the 1990s. But what that moment in the Sussex University

Meeting House showed me is that it's all been for a purpose. And it is to help those charged with telling evidence-based stories do a better job with the persuasiveness of their stories – and their use of data in meeting this objective – that I've written this book.

Thank you for your consideration.

WHERE TO FIND OUT MORE

BOOKS

Anderson, Chris (2016) *TED Talks: The Official TED Guide to Public Speaking*. Headline.

Baker, Tom (1998) *Who on Earth Is Tom Baker? An Autobiography*. HarperCollins.

Baron-Cohen, Simon (2003) *The Essential Difference: Men, Women and the Extreme Male Brain*. Penguin.

Blackmore, Susan (1999) *The Meme Machine*. Oxford University Press.

Campbell, Joseph (1949) *The Hero with a Thousand Faces*. New World Library.

Carnegie, Dale (1915/2017) *The Art of Public Speaking*. Dover Publications.

Dubner, Stephen, & Steven Levitt (2014) *Think Like a Freak: How to Think Smarter About Almost Everything*. Allen Lane.

Field, Andy (2016) *An Adventure in Statistics: The Reality Enigma*. Sage Publications.

Greenfield, Susan (2015) *Mind Change: How Digital Technologies Are Leaving Their Mark on Our Brains*. Rider.

Heath, Chip, & Dan Heath (2008) *Made to Stick: Why Some Ideas Take Hold and Others Come Unstuck*. Arrow.

Kahneman, Daniel (2011). *Thinking, Fast and Slow*. Penguin.

Mayer-Schönberger, Viktor, & Kenneth Cukier (2013) *Big Data: A Revolution That Will Transform How We Live, Work, and Think*. John Murray.

McCandless, David (2009) *Information Is Beautiful*. HarperCollins.

McCandless, David (2014) *Knowledge Is Beautiful*. HarperCollins.

McKee, Robert (1999) *Story: Substance, Structure, Style, and the Principles of Screen-writing*. Methuen.

Nussbaumer-Knaflic, Cole (2015) *Storytelling with Data: A Data Visualization Guide for Business Professionals*. John Wiley & Sons.

Pink, Daniel H. (2011) *Drive*. Cannongate Books.

Pink, Daniel H. (2014) *To Sell Is Human*. Cannongate Books.

Pinker, Steven (1999) *How the Mind Works*. Penguin.

Pinker, Steven (2014) *A Sense of Style: The Thinking Person's Guide to Writing in the 21st Century*. Allen Lane.

Ronson, Jon (2011) *The Psychopath Test: A Journey Through the Madness Industry*. Picador.

Silver, Nate (2013) *The Signal & the Noise*. Penguin.

Simmons, John (2000) *We, Me, Them, and It*. Urbane Publications.

Simmons, John (2003) *The Invisible Grail*. Texere Publishing.

Simmons, John (2004) *Dark Angels*. Urbane Publications.

Sinek, Simon (2009) *Start with Why: How Great Leaders Inspire Everyone to Take Action*. Penguin.

Snow, C.P. (1959) *The Two Cultures and the Scientific Revolution: The Rede Lecture 1959*. Cambridge University Press.

Tasgal, Anthony (2015) *The Storytelling Book*. LID Publishing.

Tufte, Edward (2001) *The Visual Display of Quantitative Information*. Graphics Press.

Tufte, Edward (2006) *The Cognitive Style of PowerPoint: Pitching Out Corrupts within*. Graphics Press.

Vigen, Tyler (2015) *Spurious Correlations*. Hachette Books.

TED TALKS

Amanpour, Christiane, in Conversation with TED's Chris Anderson (2017) *How to seek truth in the era of fake news*. http://bit.ly/2i6AoUV

Chalabi, Mona (2017) *3 ways to spot a bad statistic*. http://bit.ly/2mLt96d

McCandless, David (2010) *The beauty of data visualization*. http://bit.ly/1p1Njxv

Palmer, Amanda (2013) *The art of asking*. http://bit.ly/1lk3MBX

Rosling, Hans (2006) *The best stats you've ever seen*. http://bit.ly/1rP9yP8

Sinek's, Simon (2009) *How great leaders inspire action (aka "start with 'why?'")*. http://bit.ly/1fQ1qY0

Treasure, Julian (2013) *How to speak so that people want to listen*. http://bit.ly/2g4RpYY

Wellington, Ben (2015) *Making data mean more through storytelling at TEDxBroadway*. http://bit.ly/1XzrMAd

And finally . . . Marillion keyboard player Mark Kelly on how the progressive rock dinosaurs from Aylesbury I grew up with only went and invented crowd-funding last millennium. A great story, compelling told, data-driven, and from a most unlikely source http://huff.to/2gKlhwo

INDEX